Infinite Ocean

AI

Copyright © 2023 Artbooks by AI

All rights reserved.

ISBN 9798375806976

Check out our other AI produced content on Amazon:
Instructional Guides By AI

I hope you enjoy the Journey Through the Forest Coloring Book as much as we do. I made the first one for myself and my kids since coloring is an activity we enjoy doing together. We had such a good time that we wanted to share the same content with others.

Questions comments or suggestions – instructionalguidesbyai@gmail.com

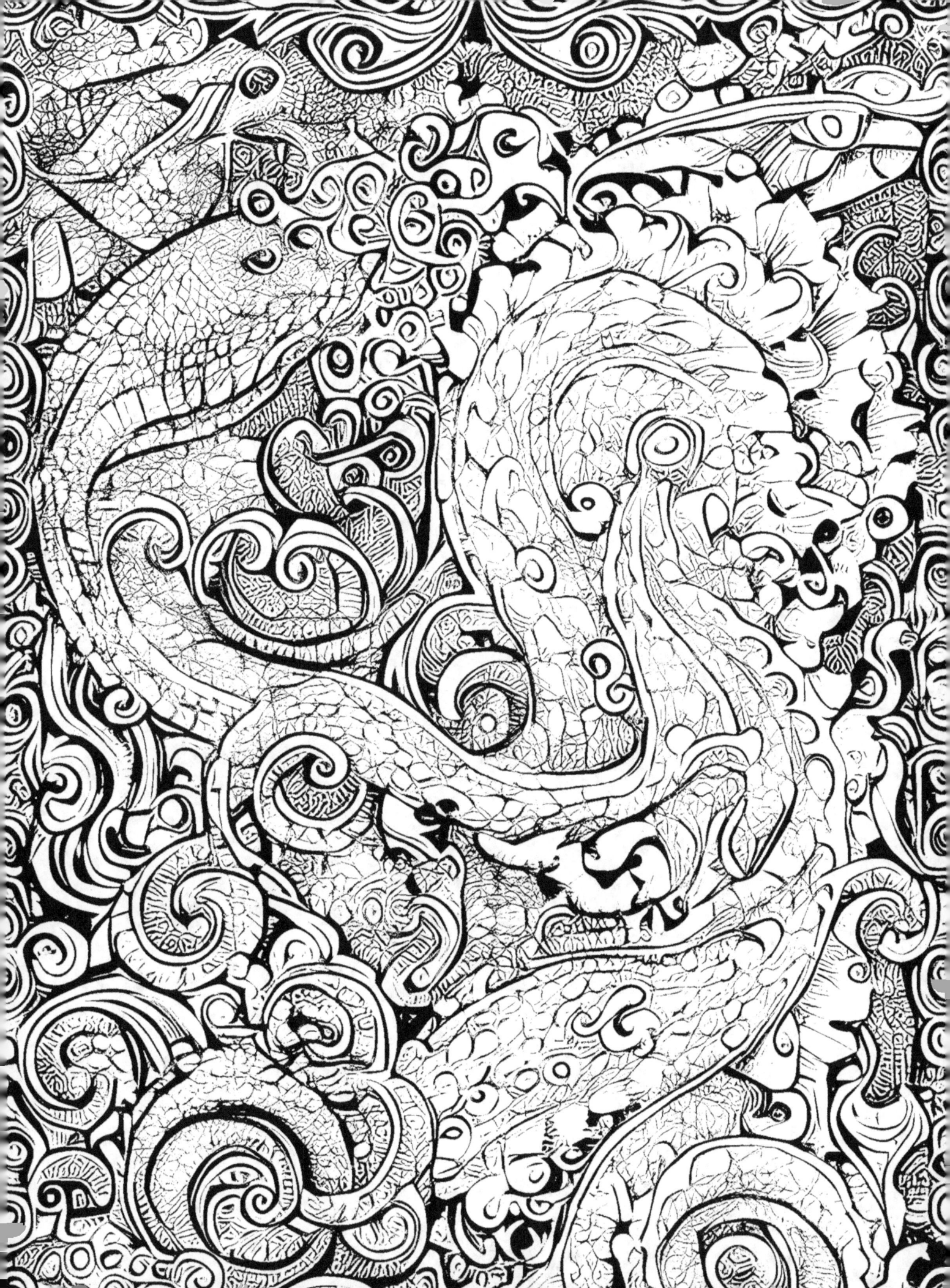

Infinite Ocean

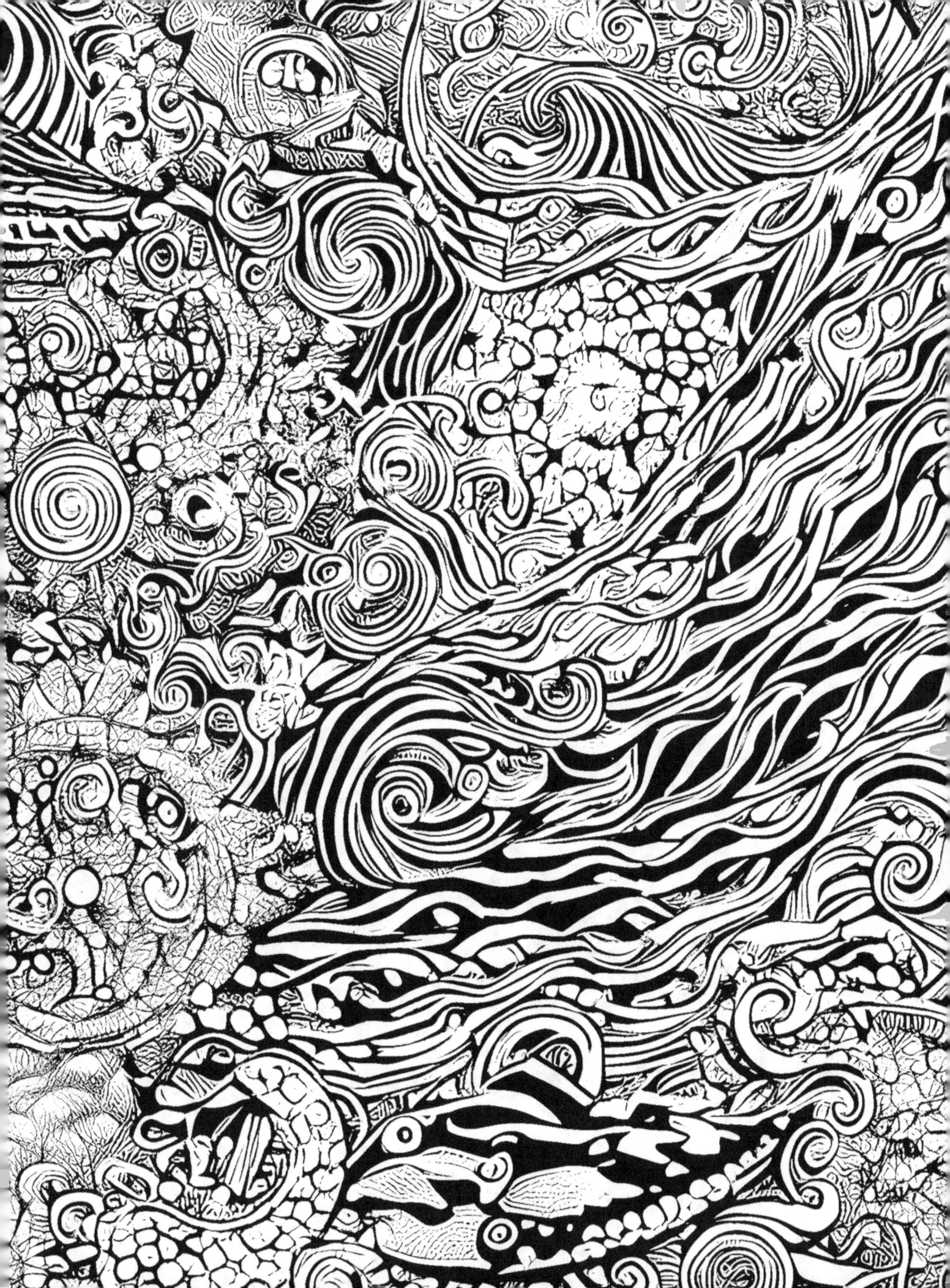

Infinite Ocean

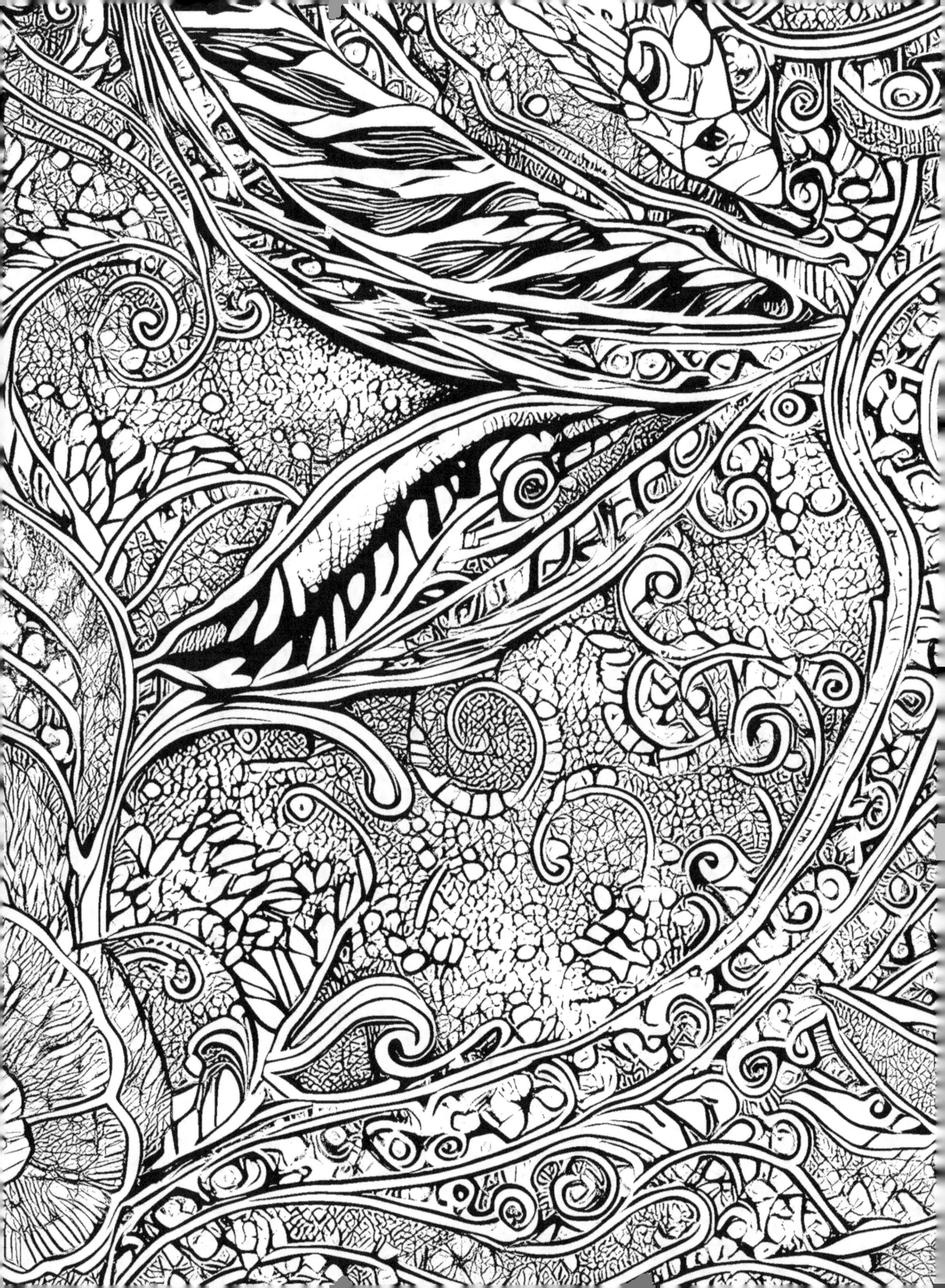

Infinite Ocean

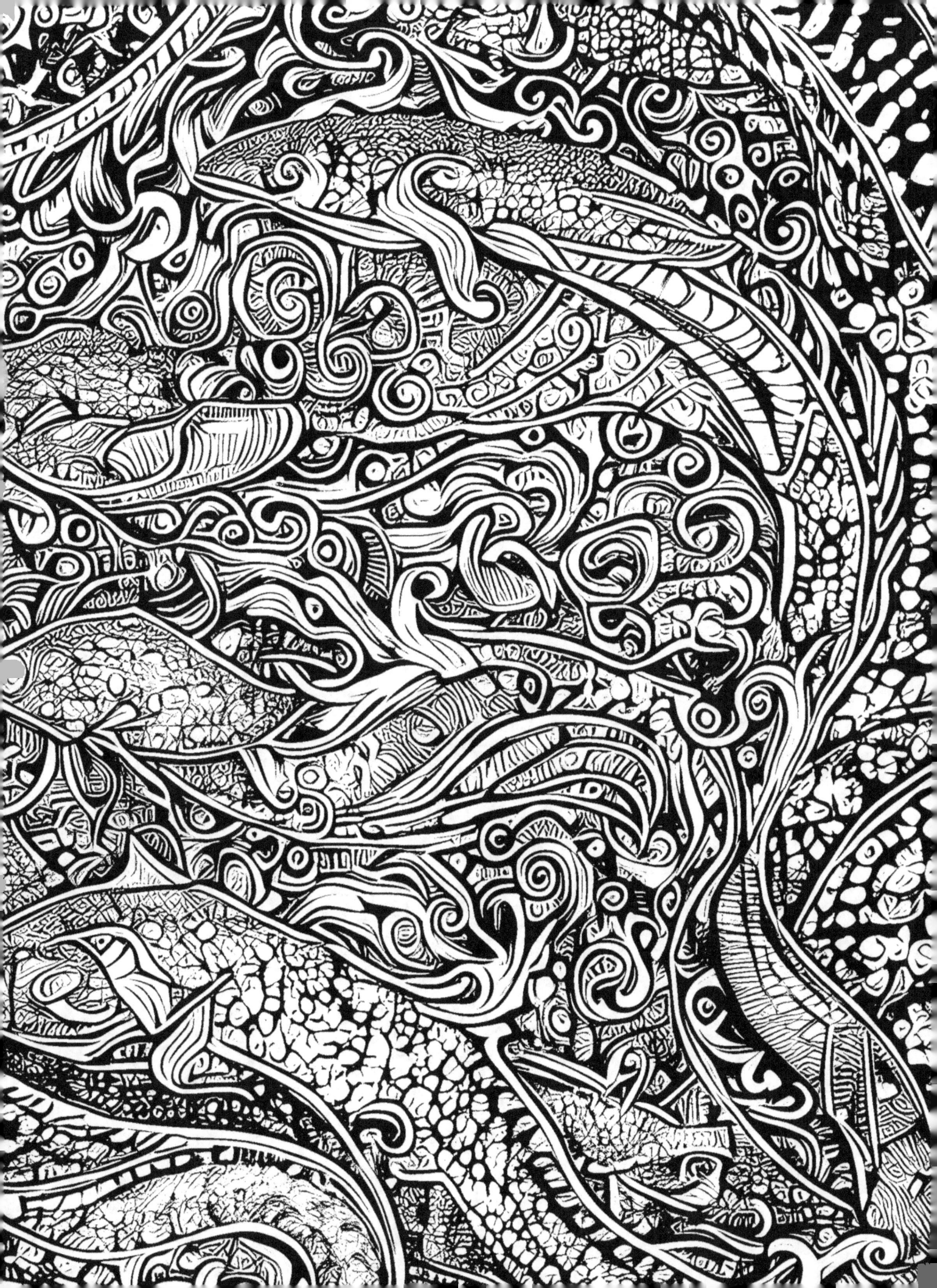

Infinite Ocean

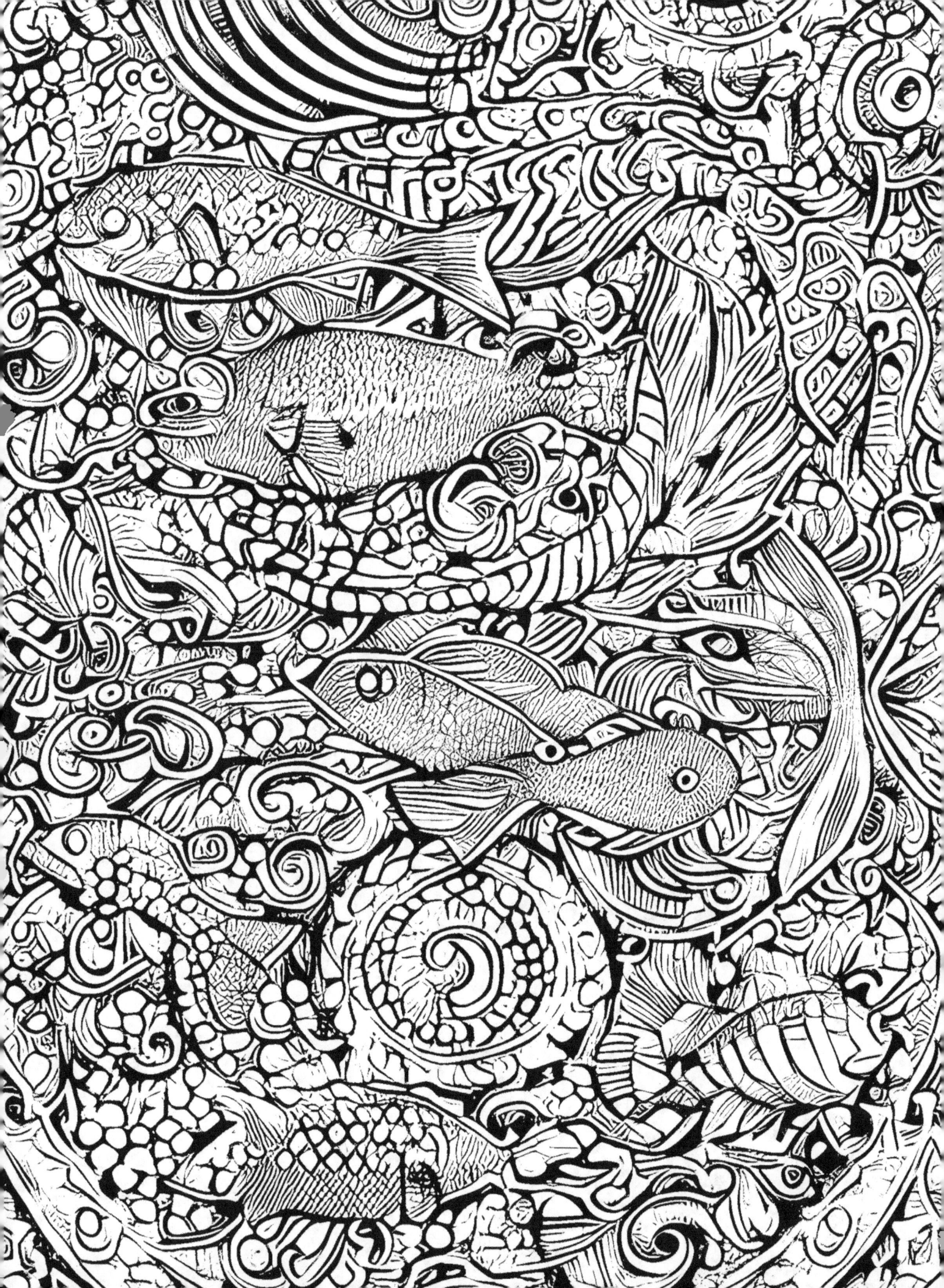

Infinite Ocean

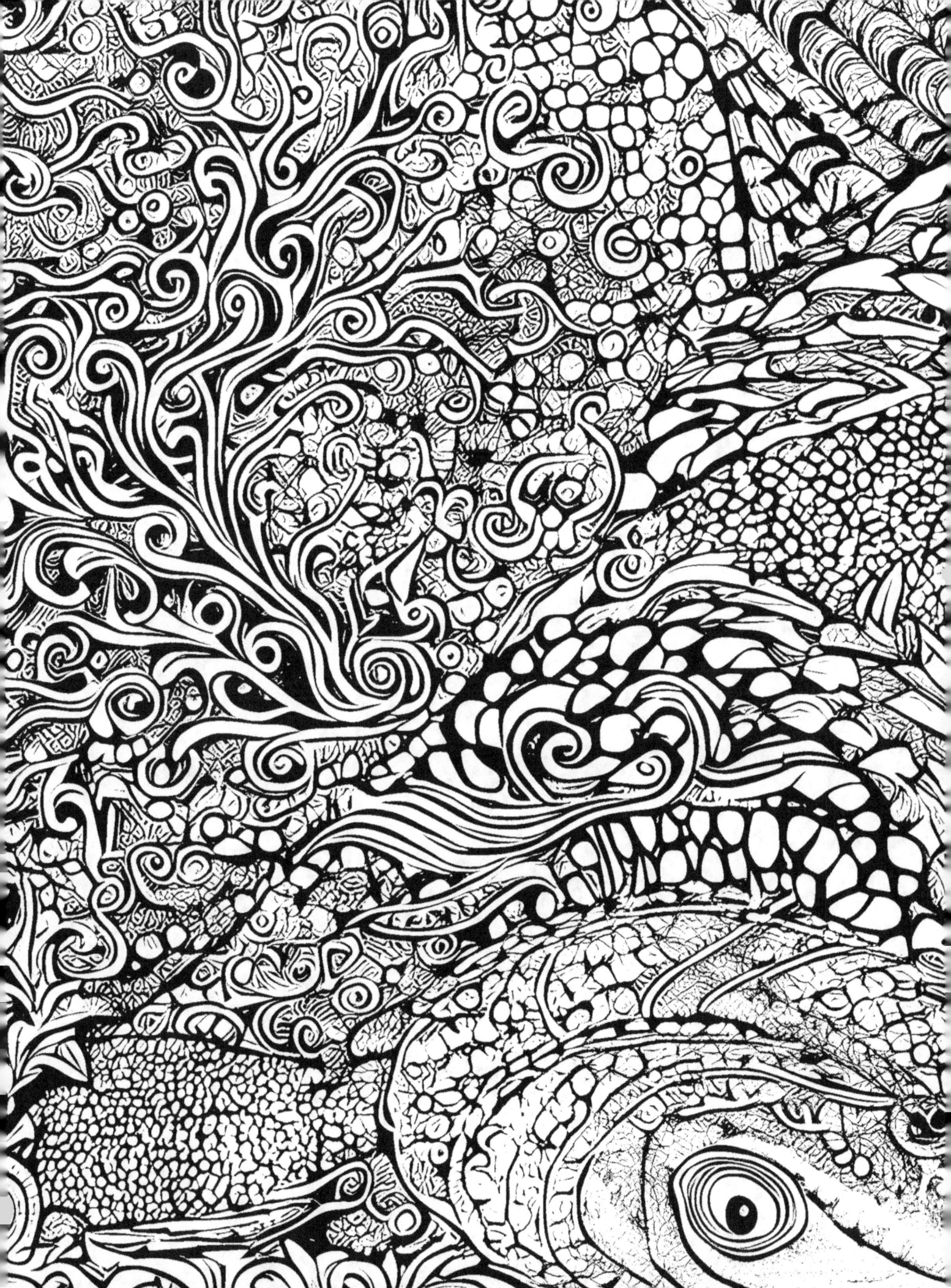

Infinite Ocean

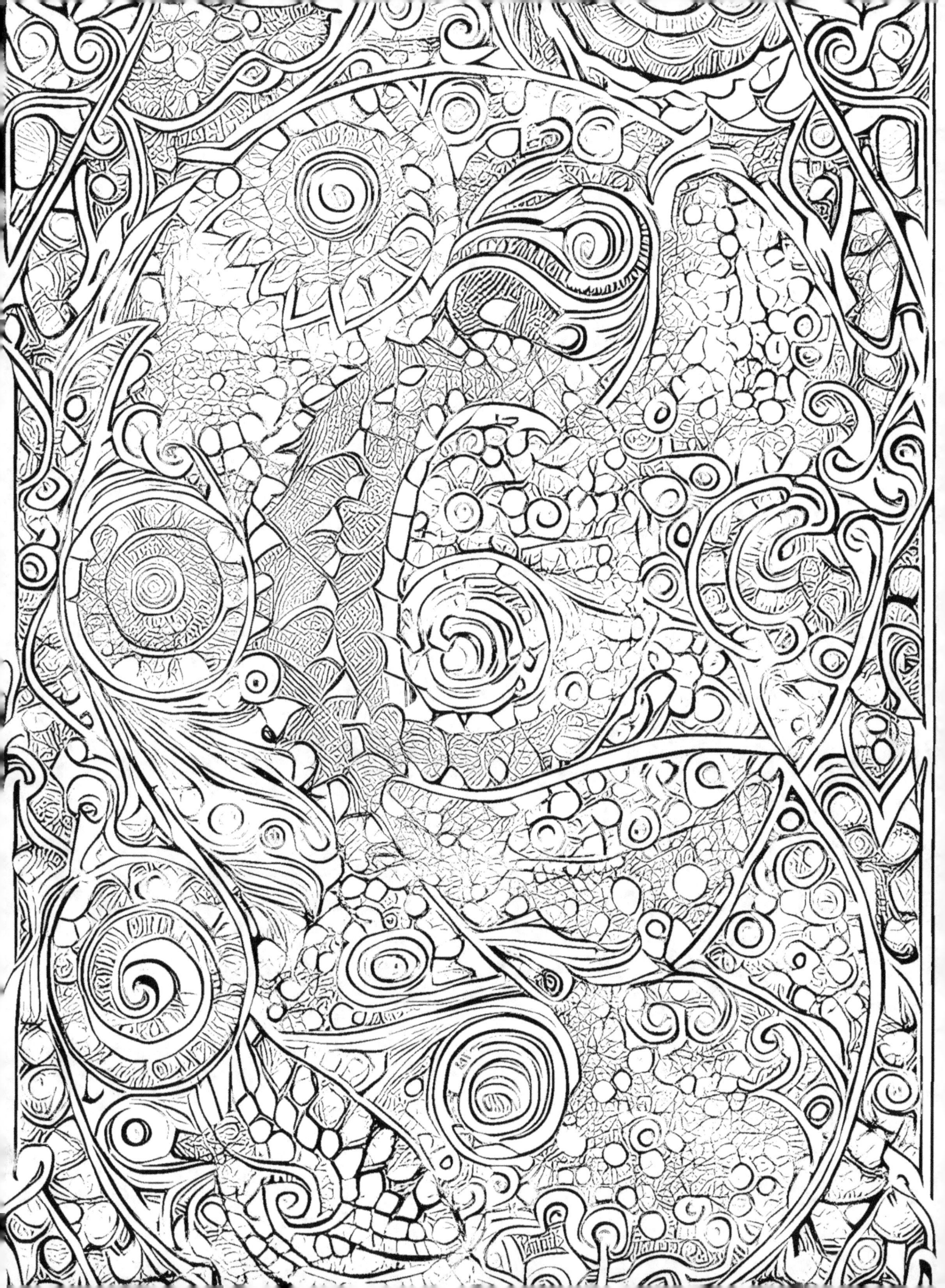

Infinite Ocean

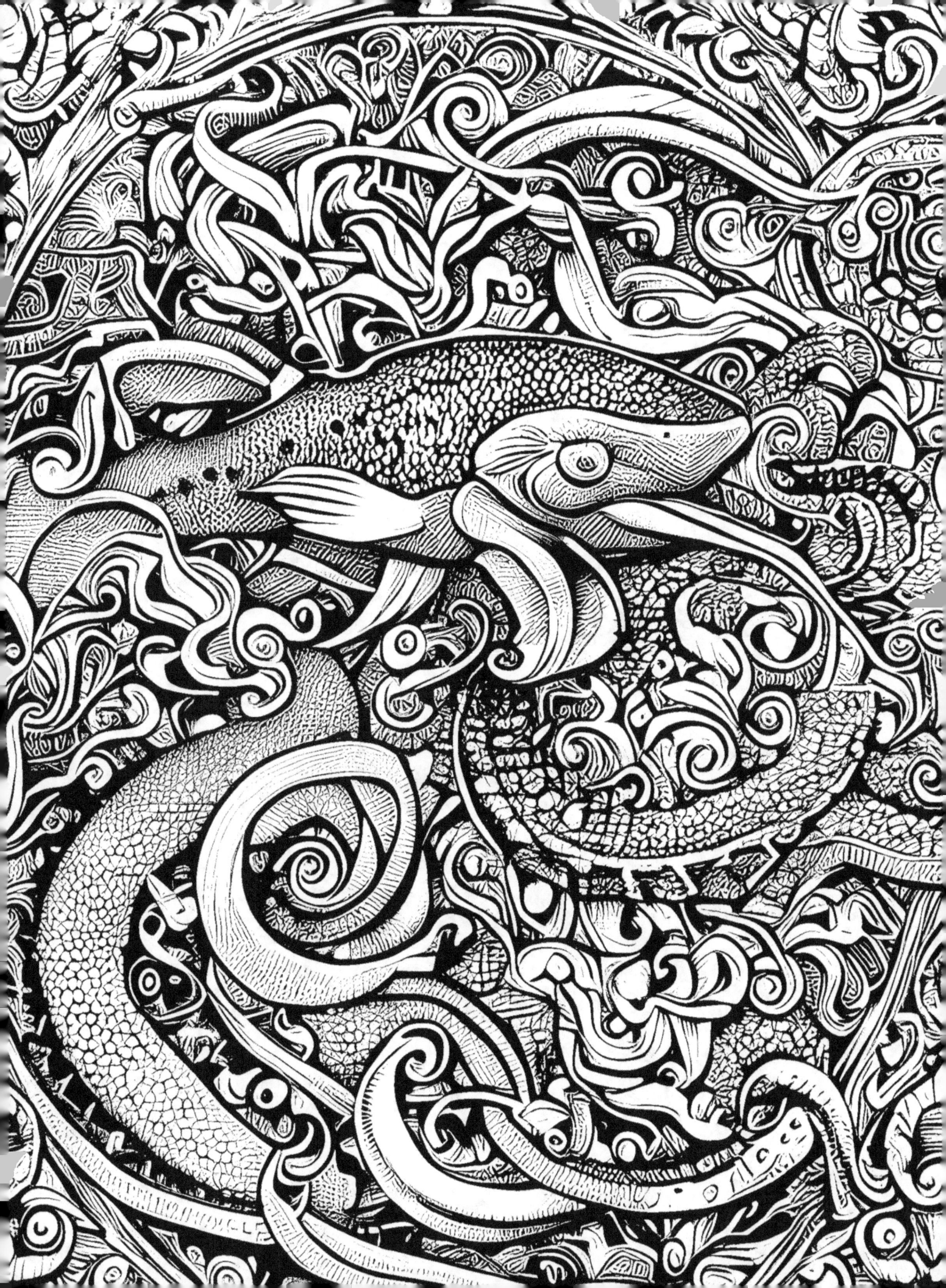

Infinite Ocean

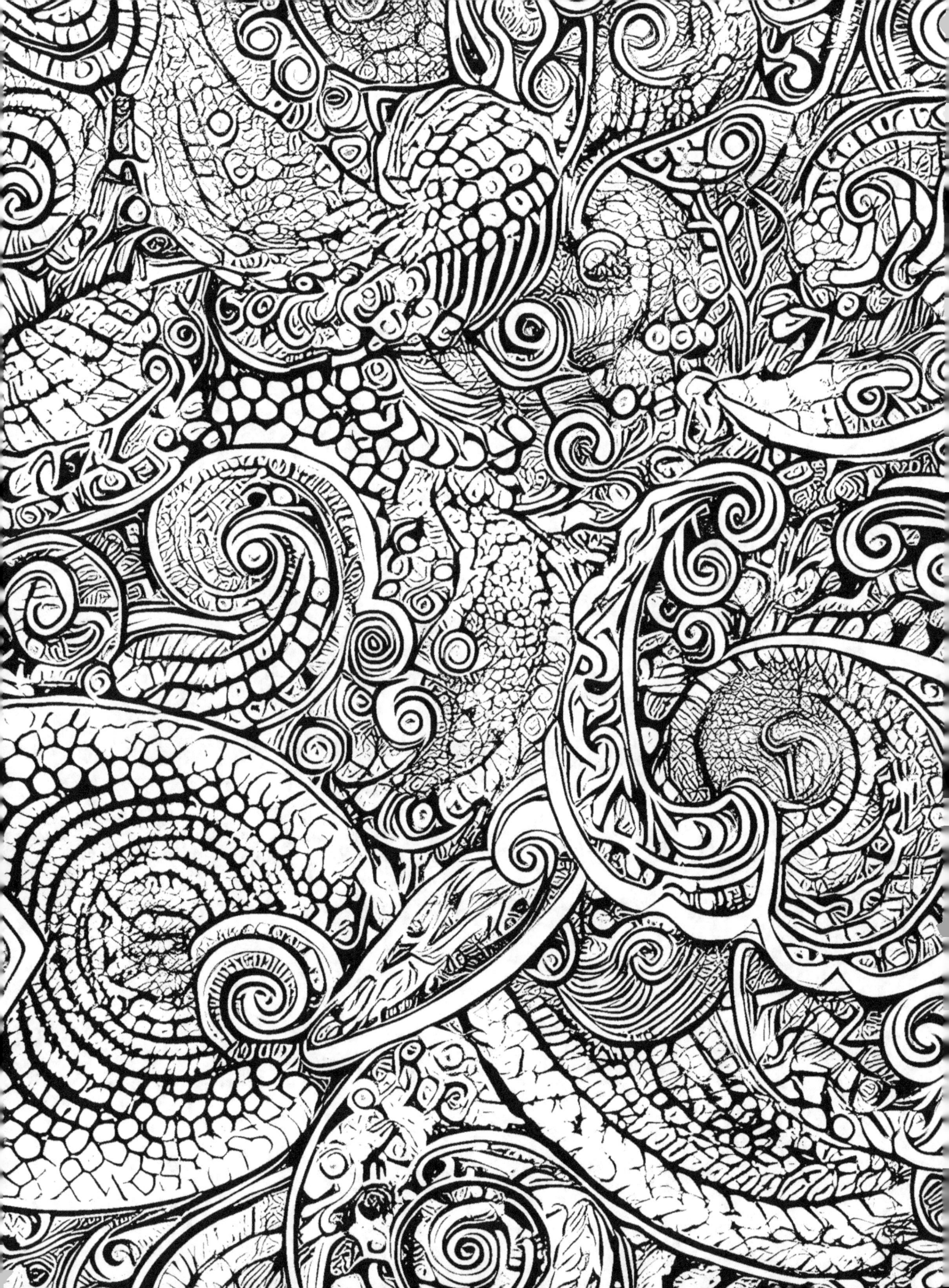

Infinite Ocean

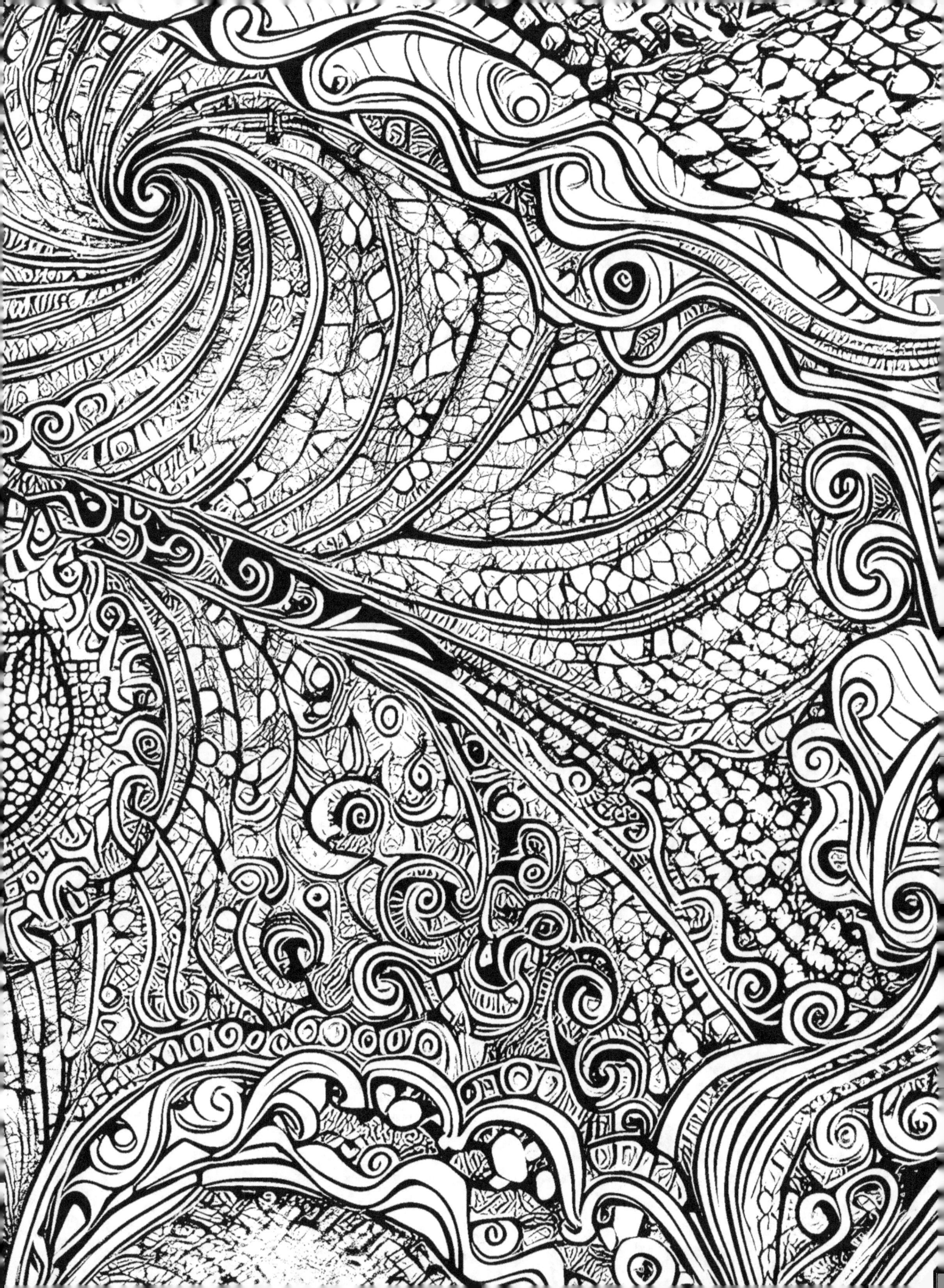

Infinite Ocean

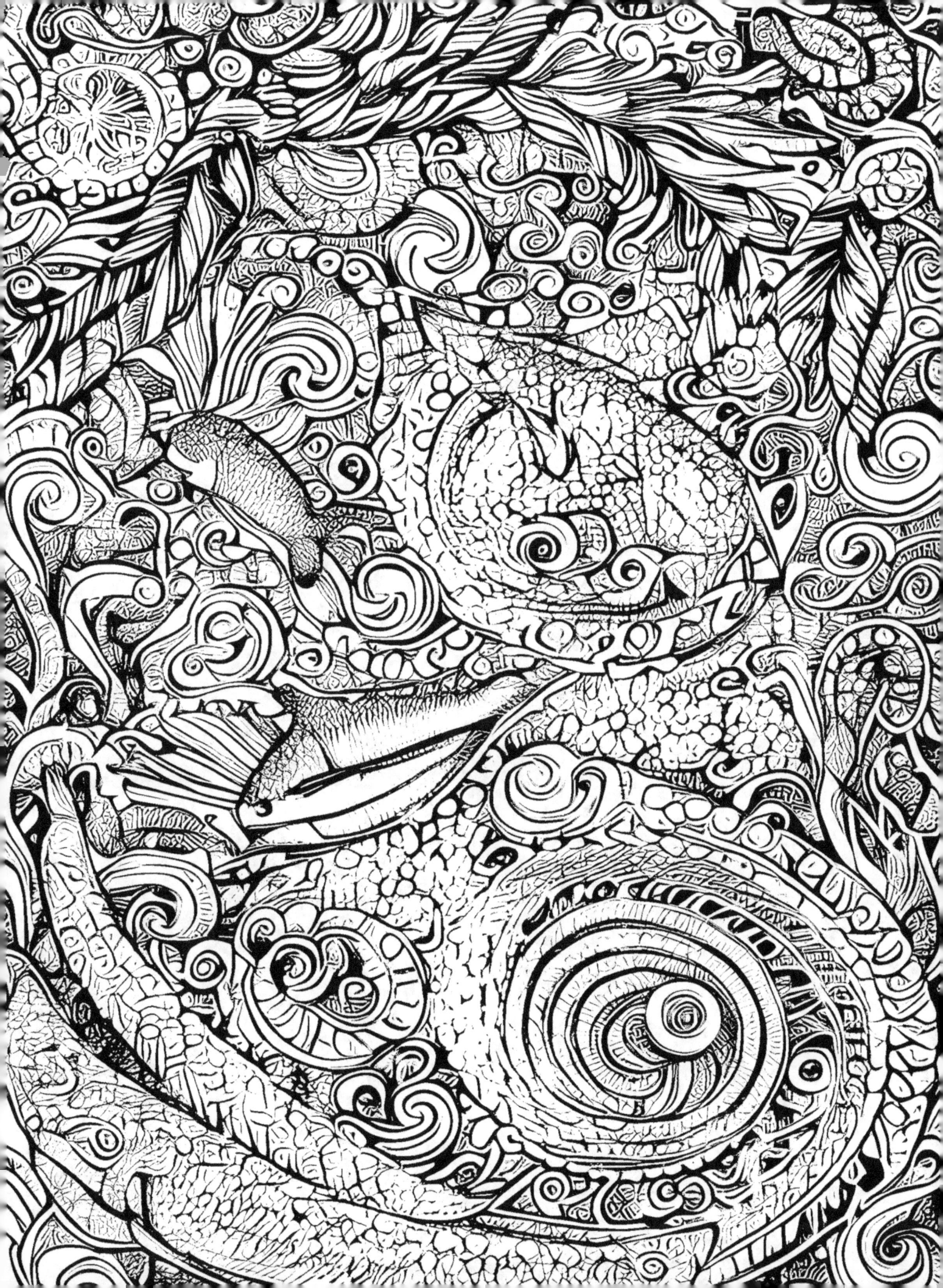

Infinite Ocean

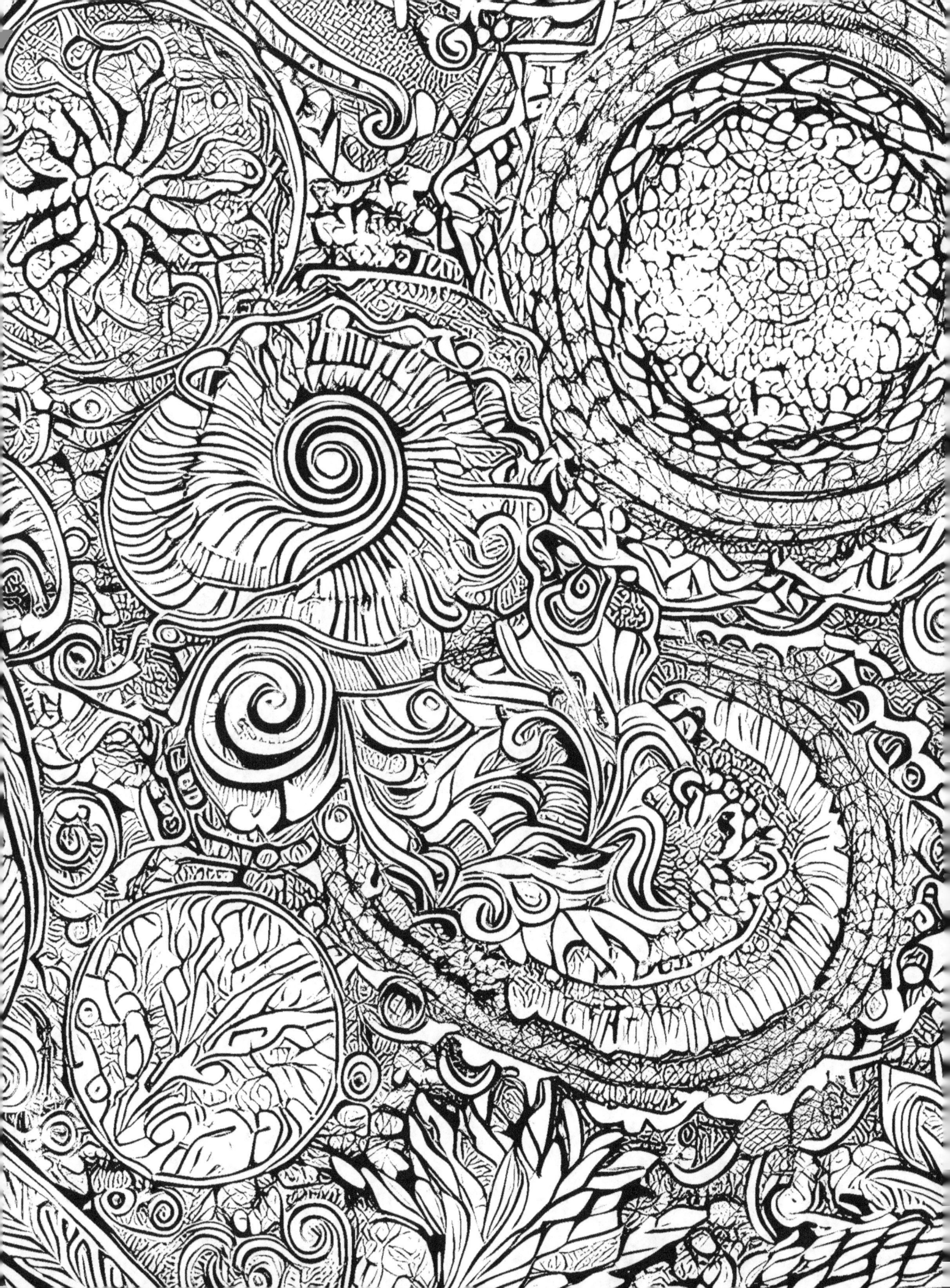

Infinite Ocean

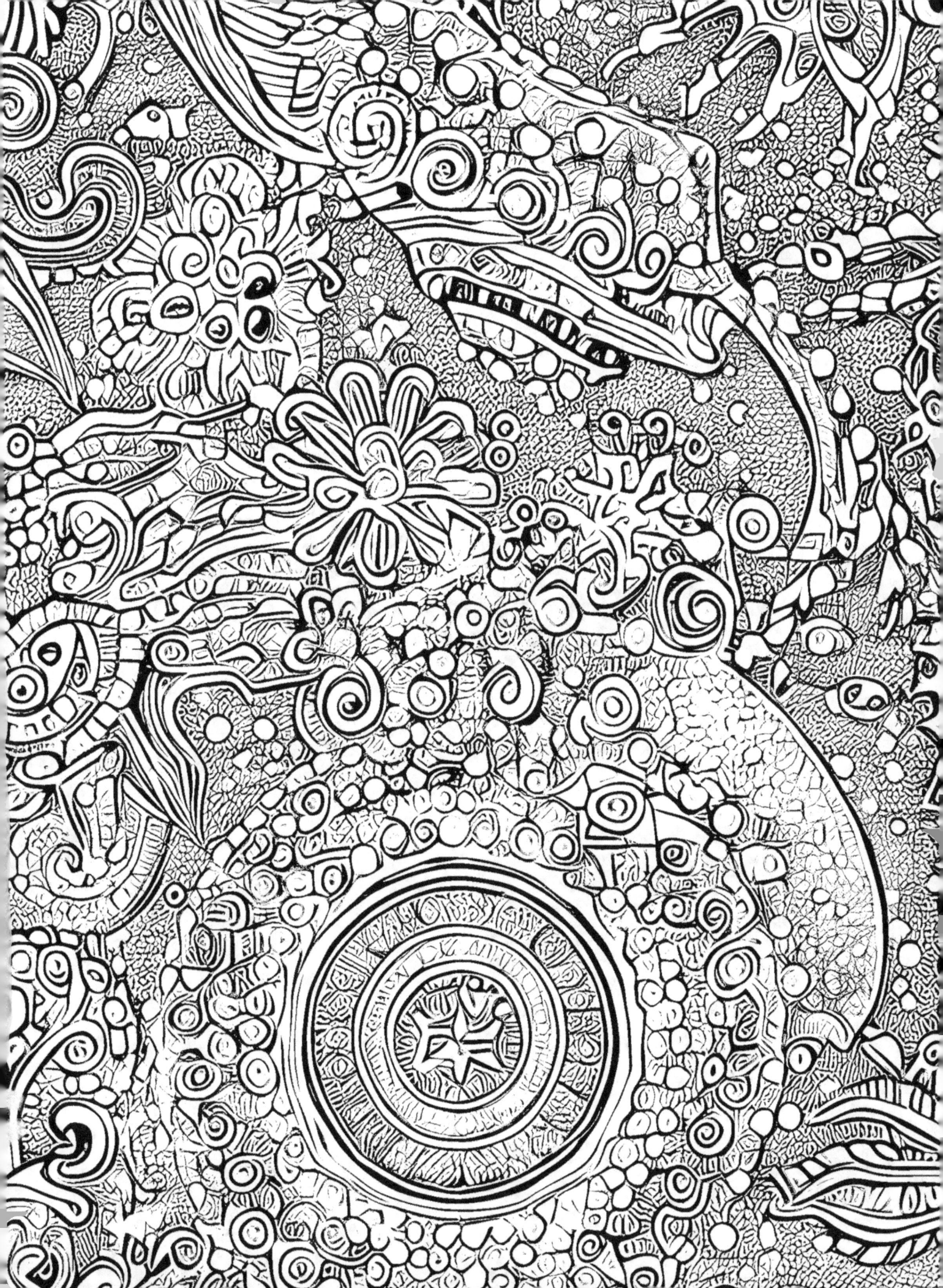

Infinite Ocean

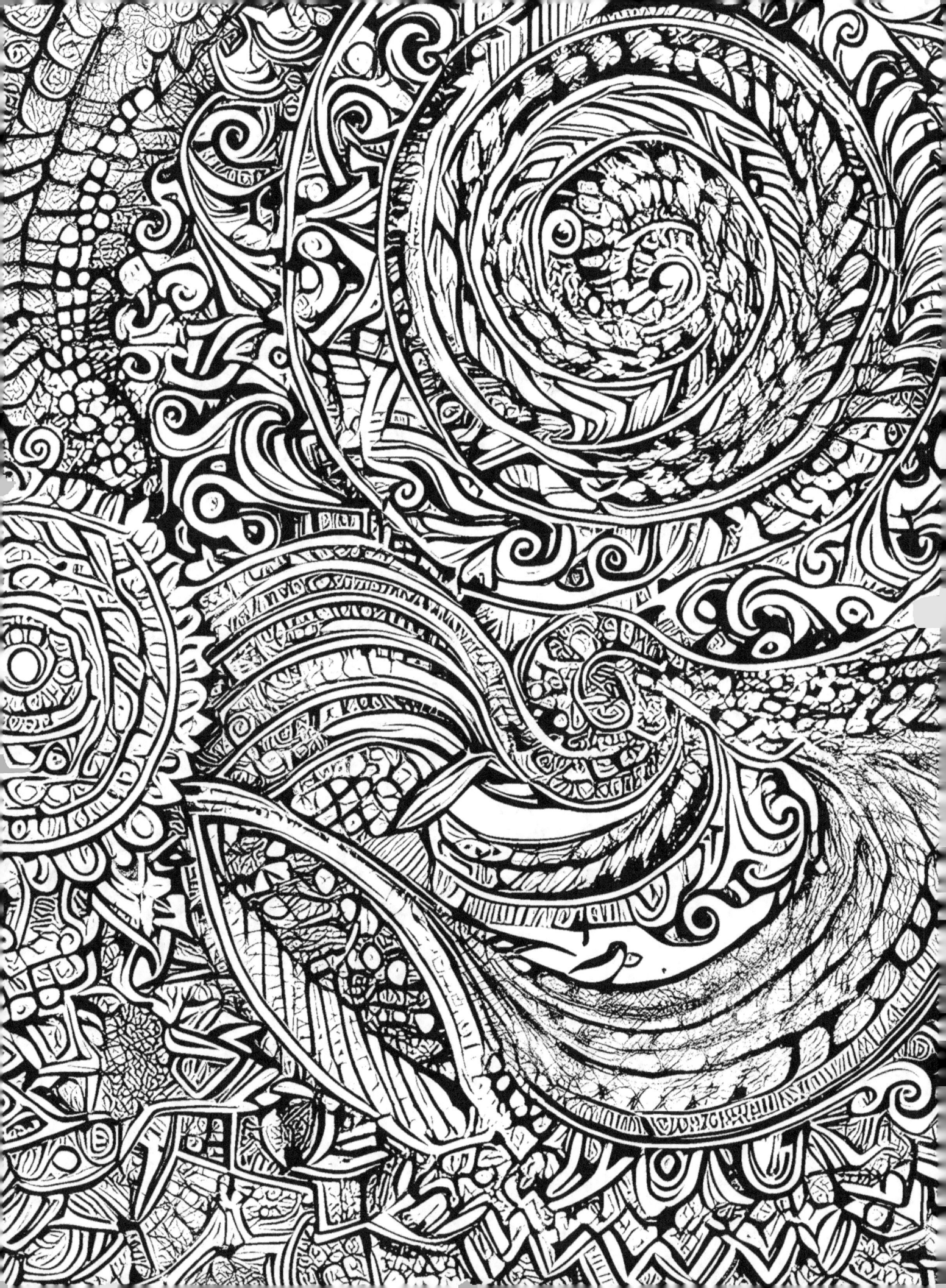

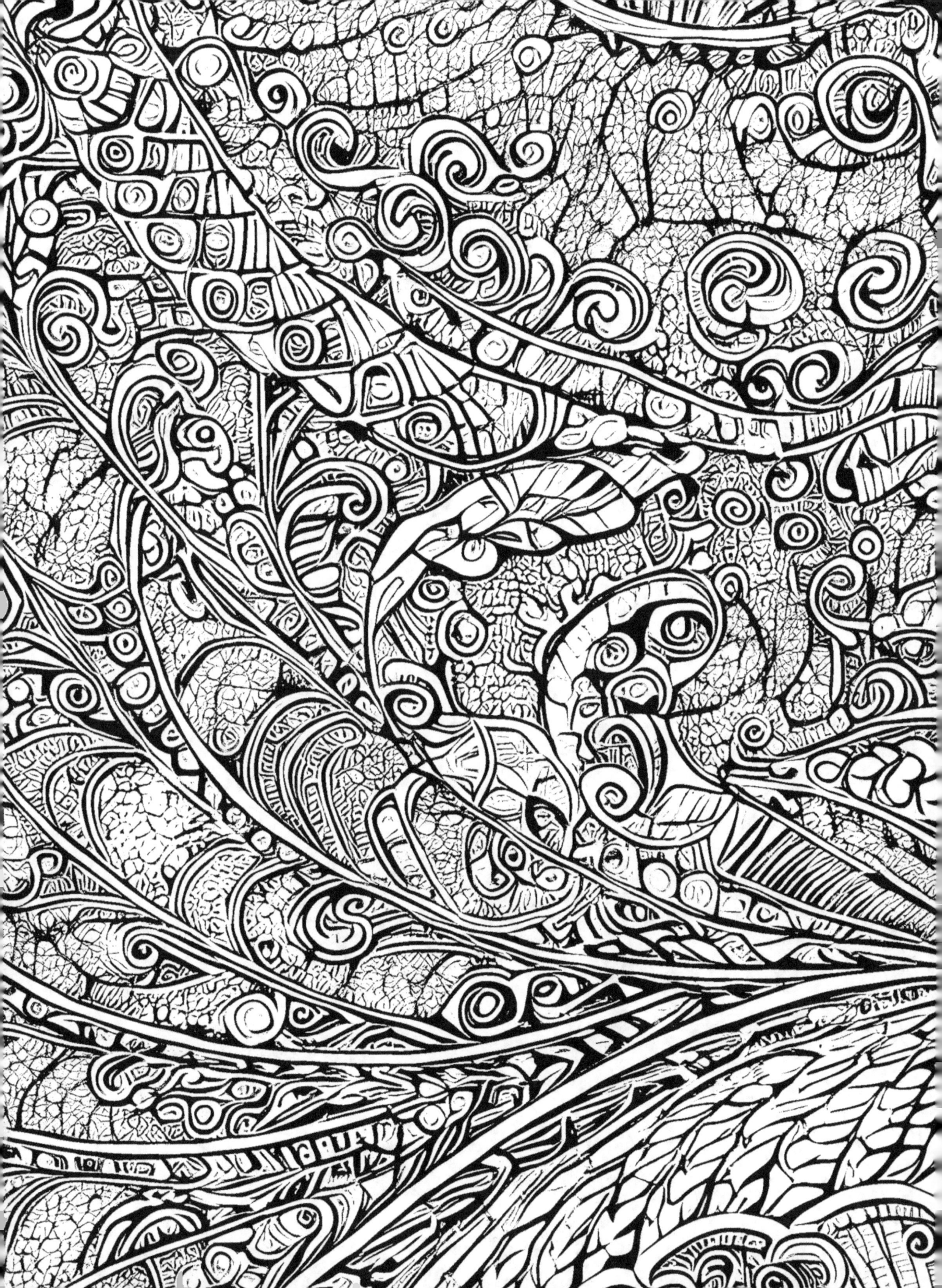

Infinite Ocean

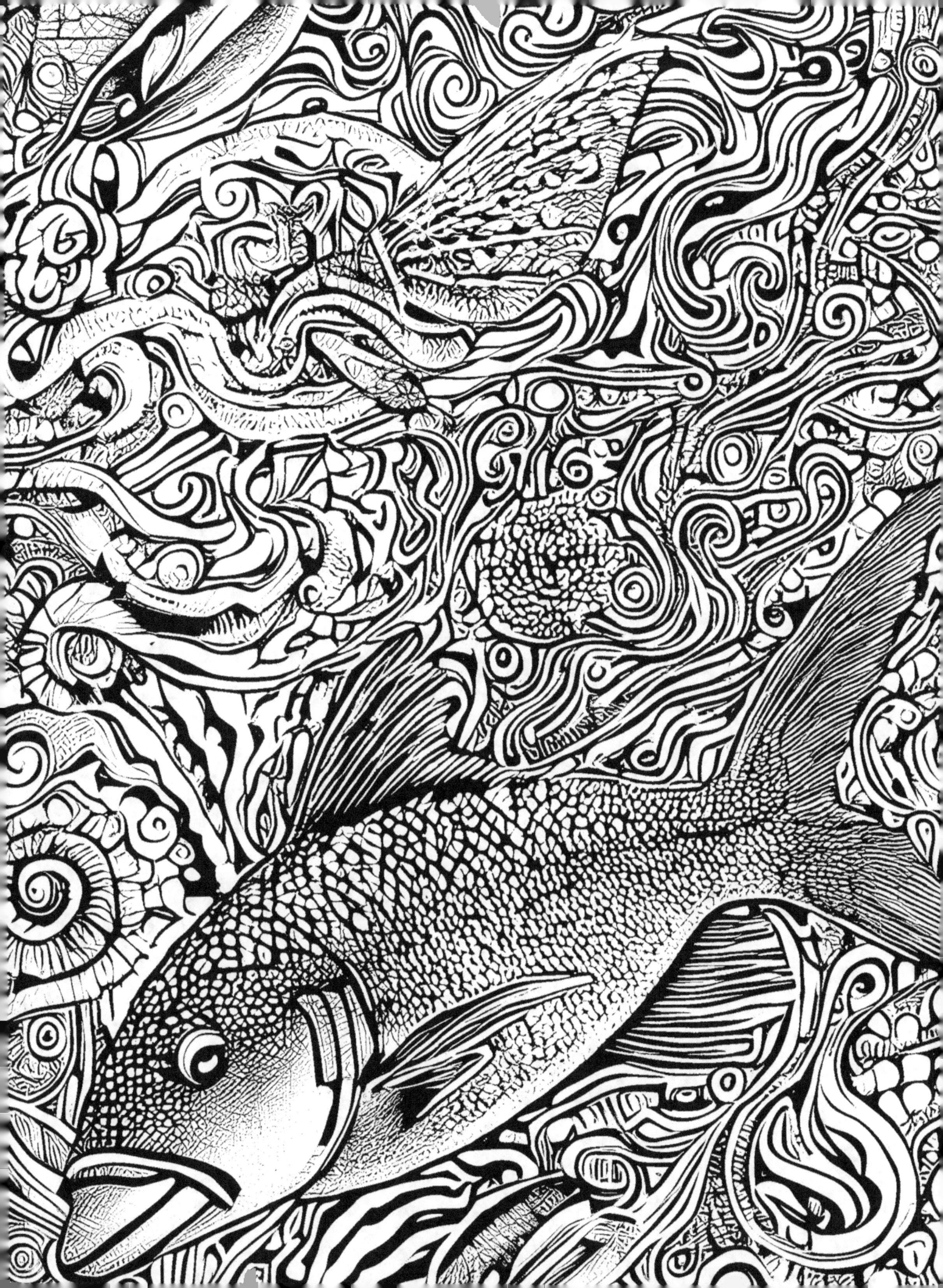

Infinite Ocean

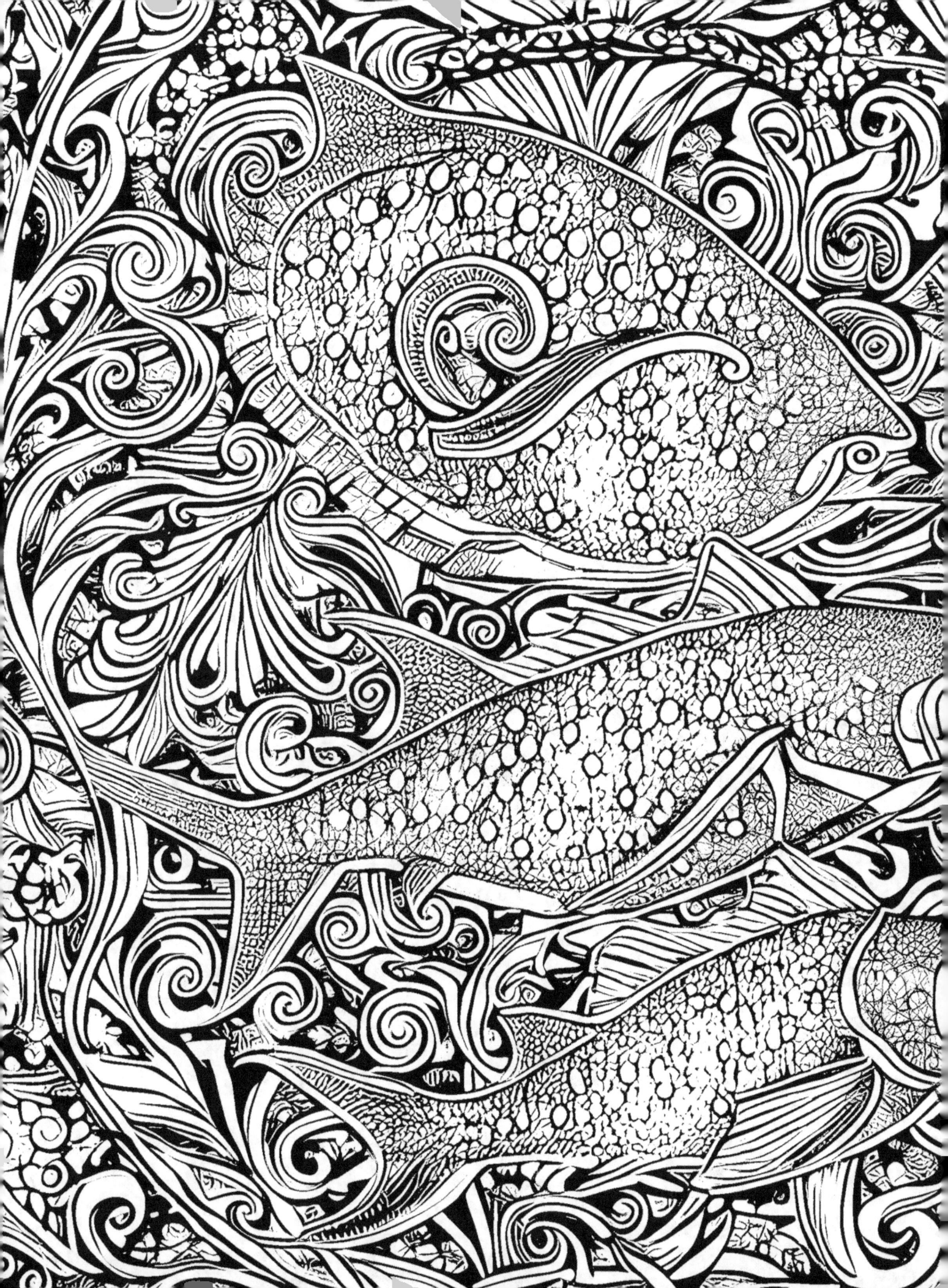

Infinite Ocean

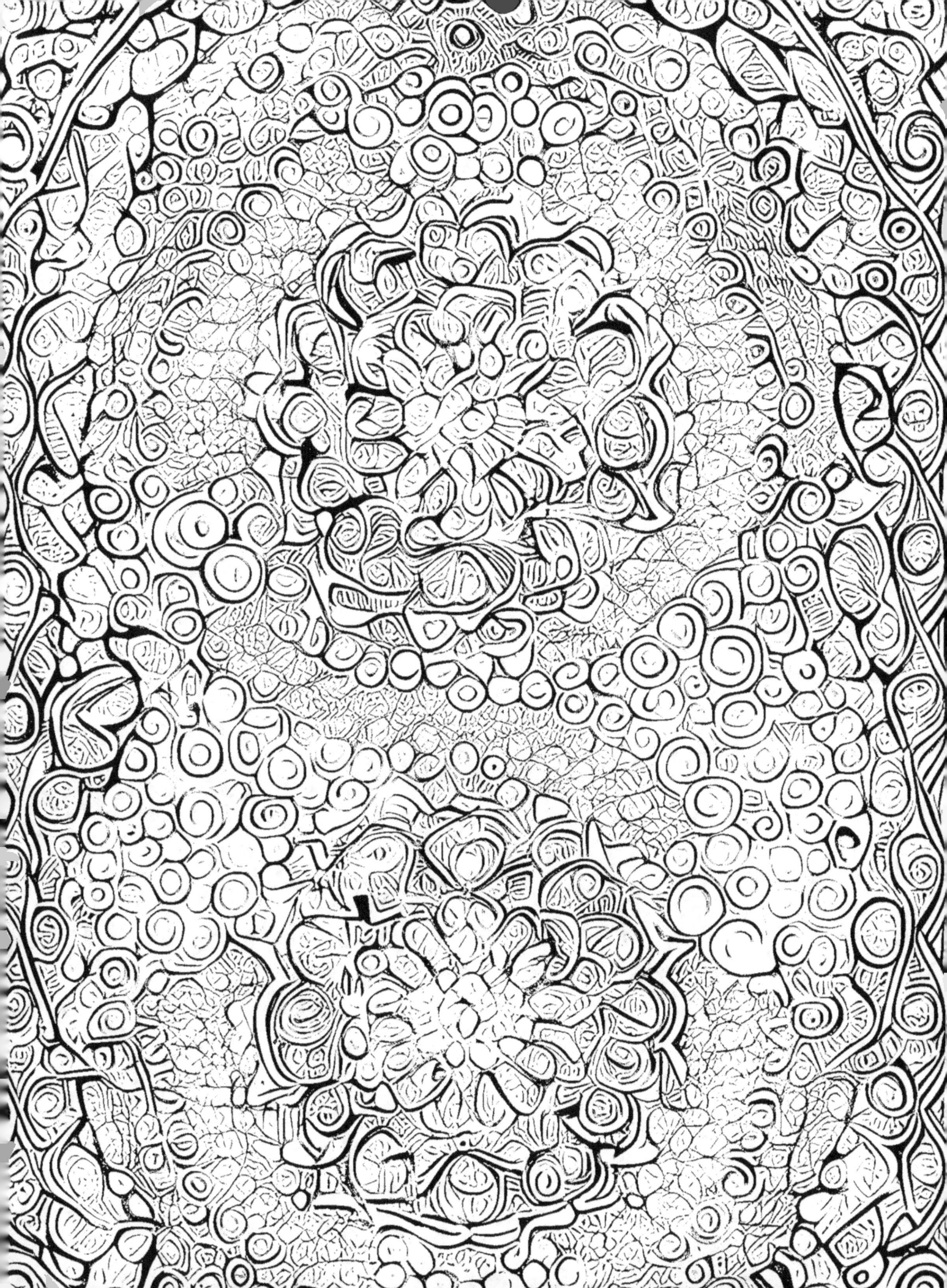

Infinite Ocean

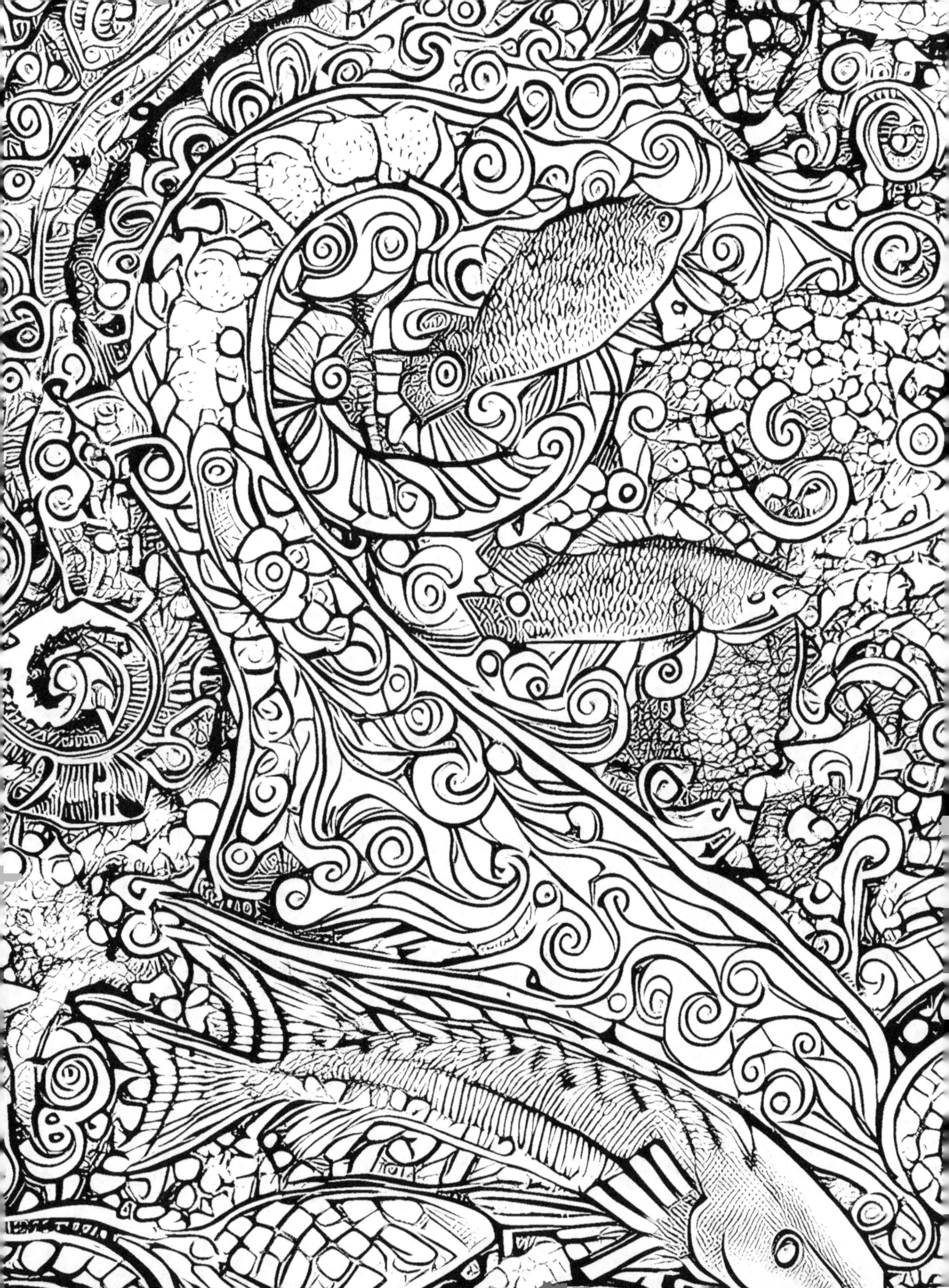

Infinite Ocean

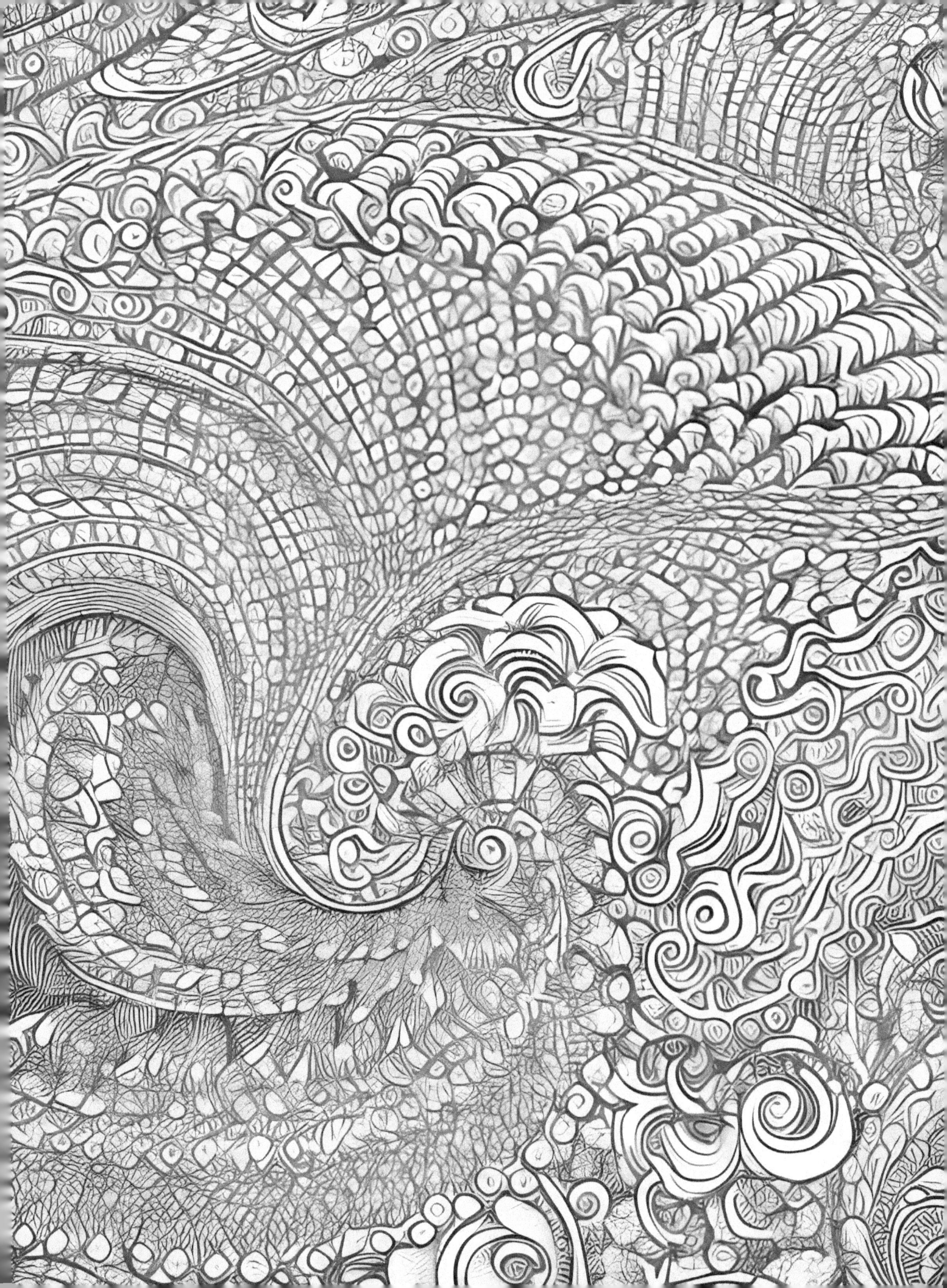

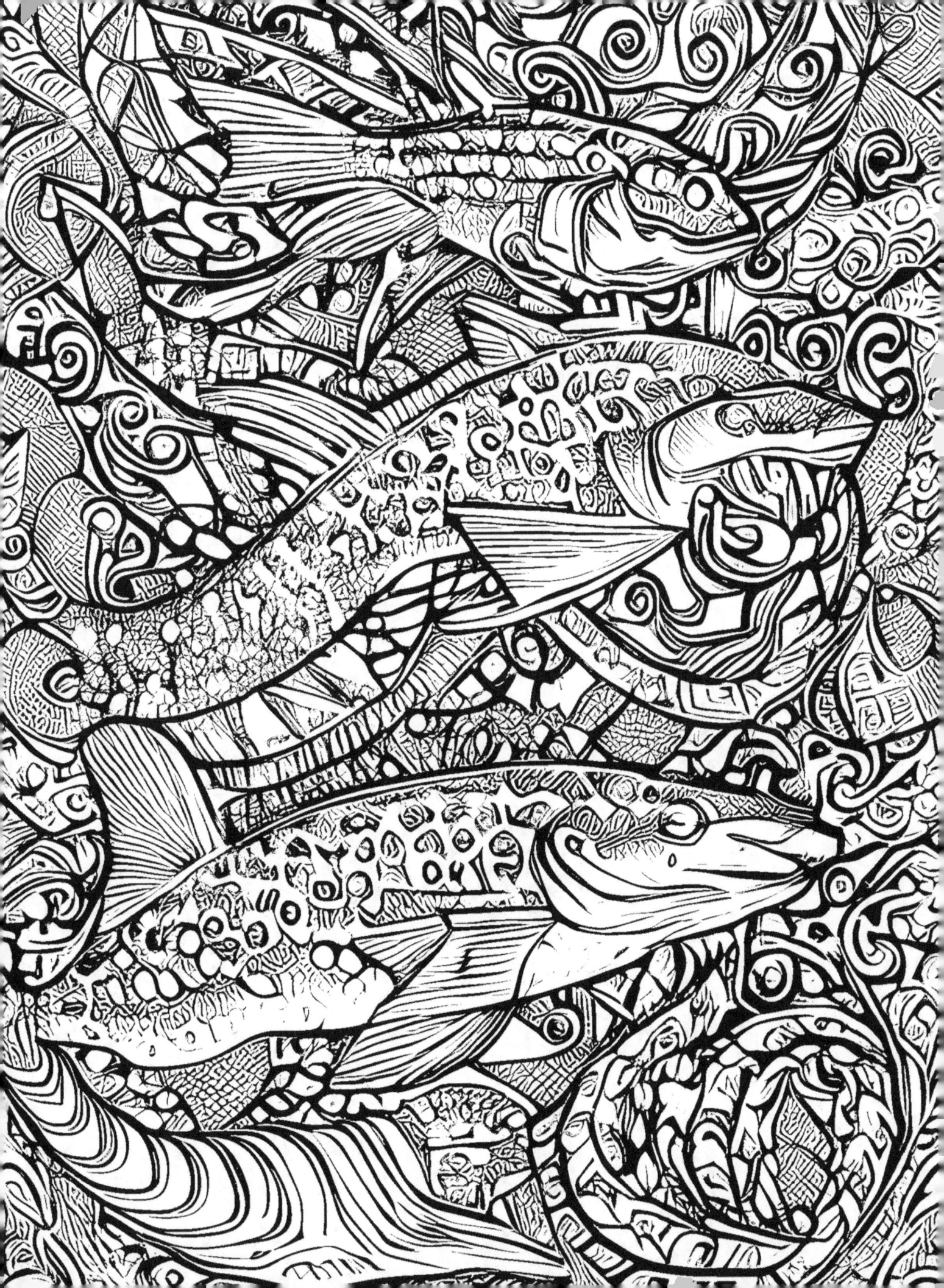

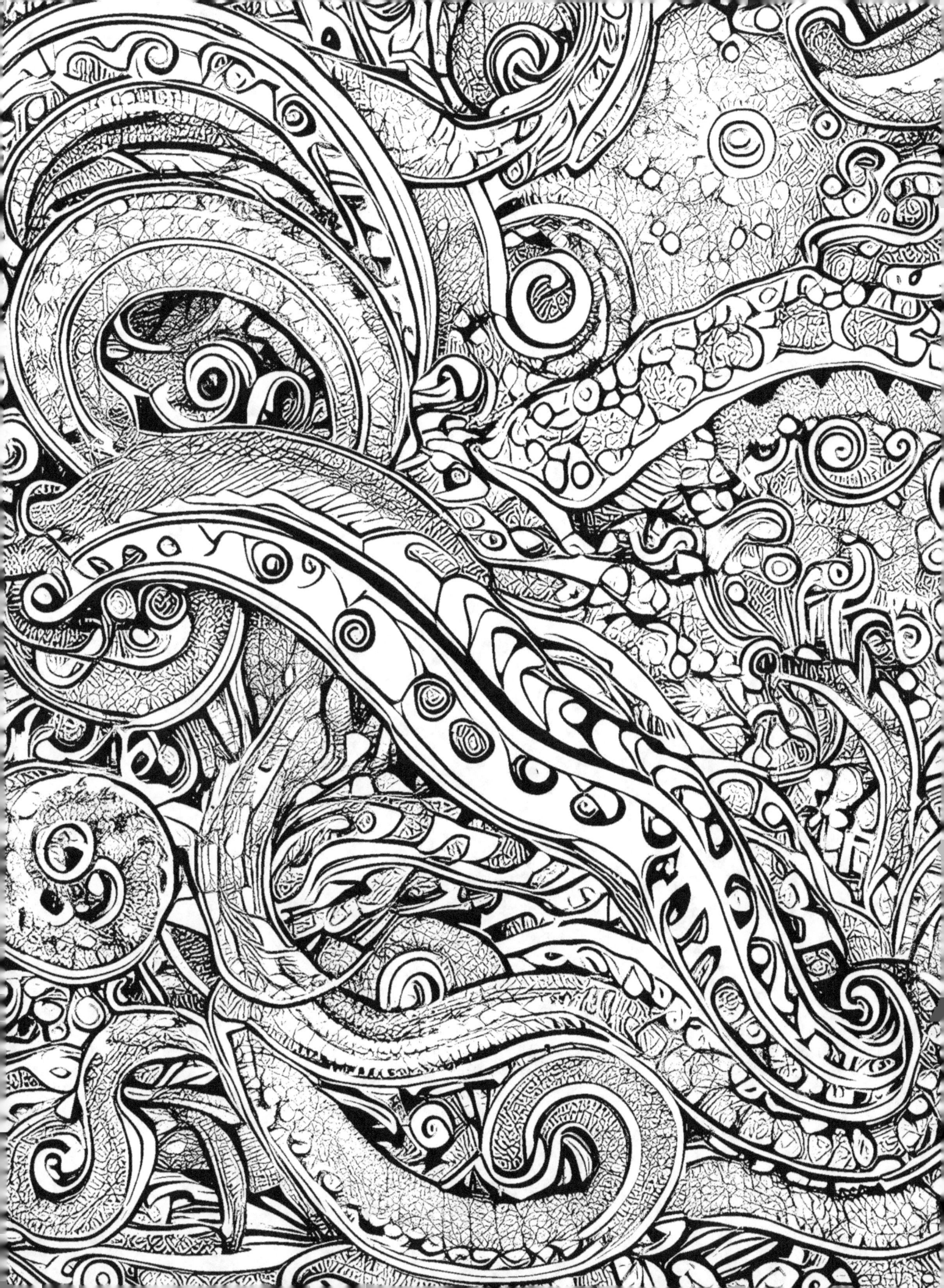

Infinite Ocean

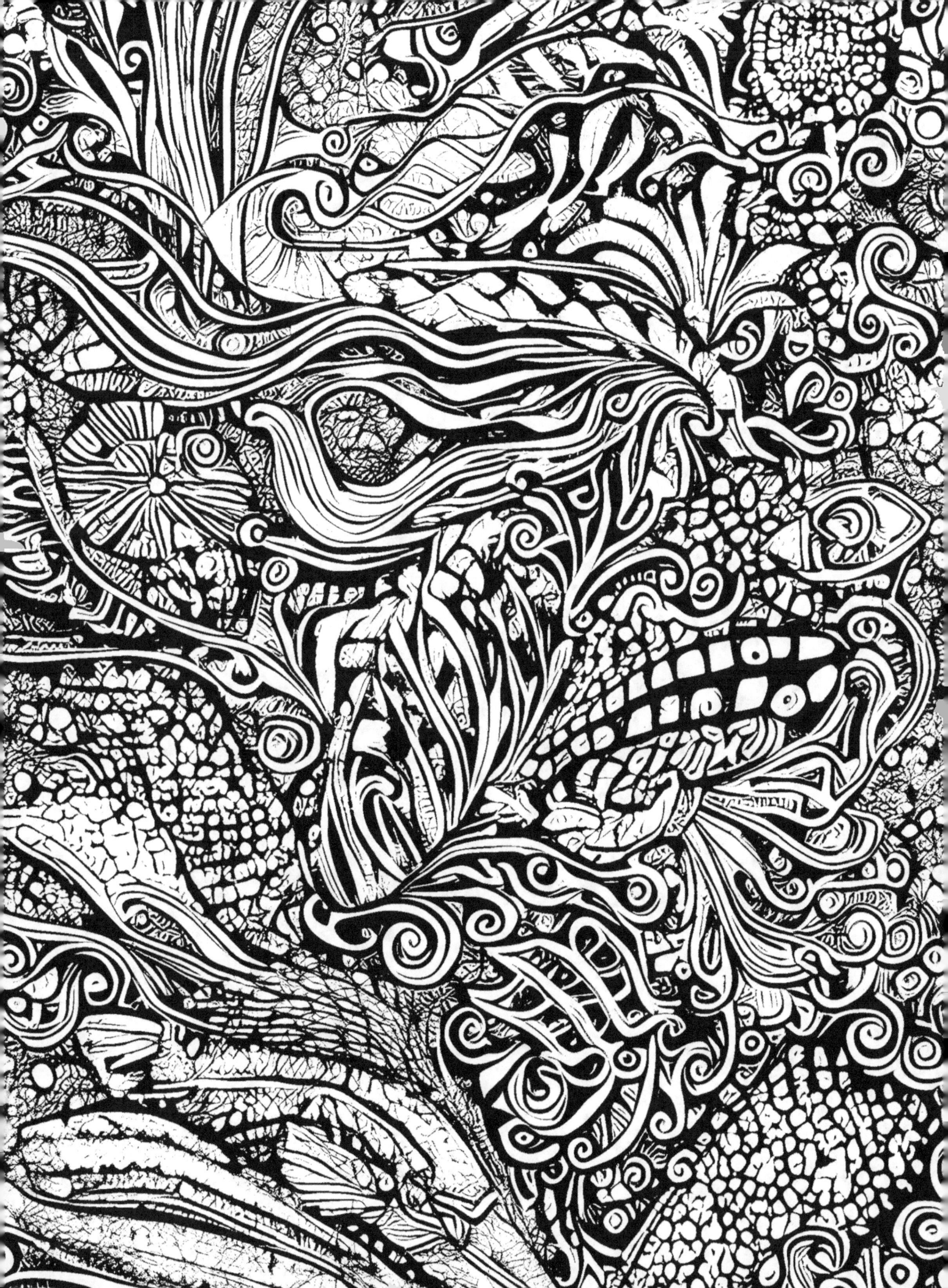

Infinite Ocean

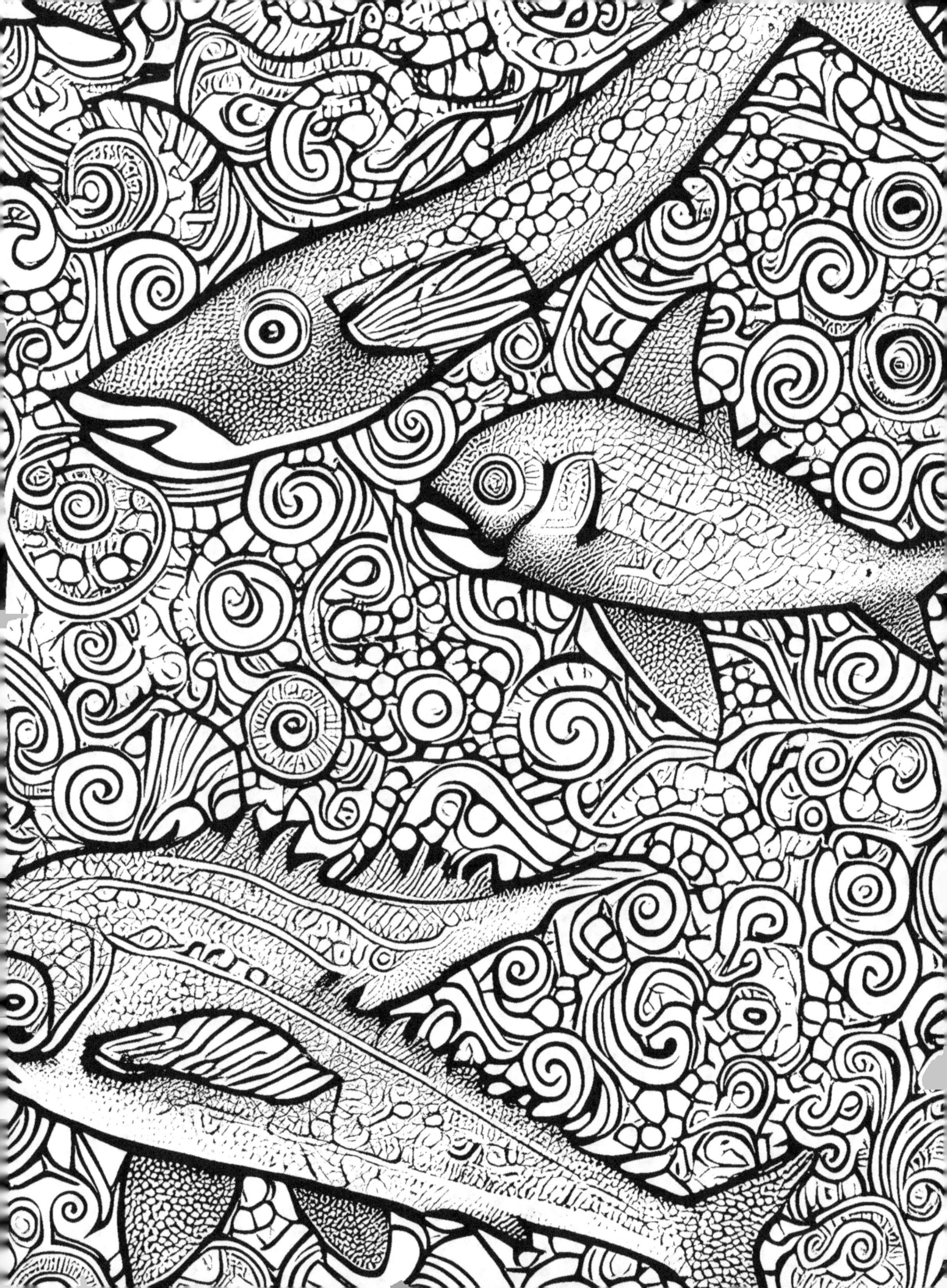

Infinite Ocean

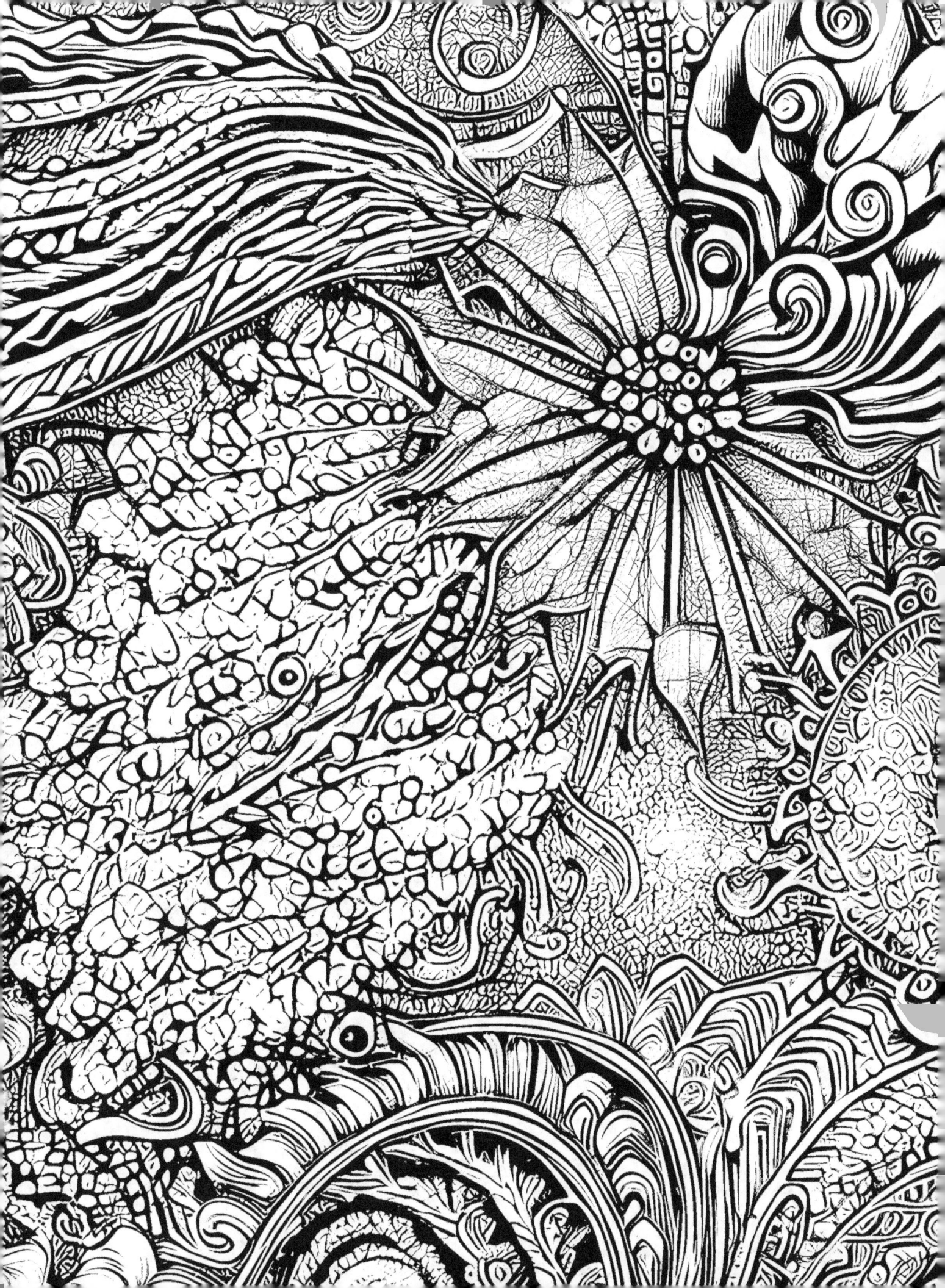

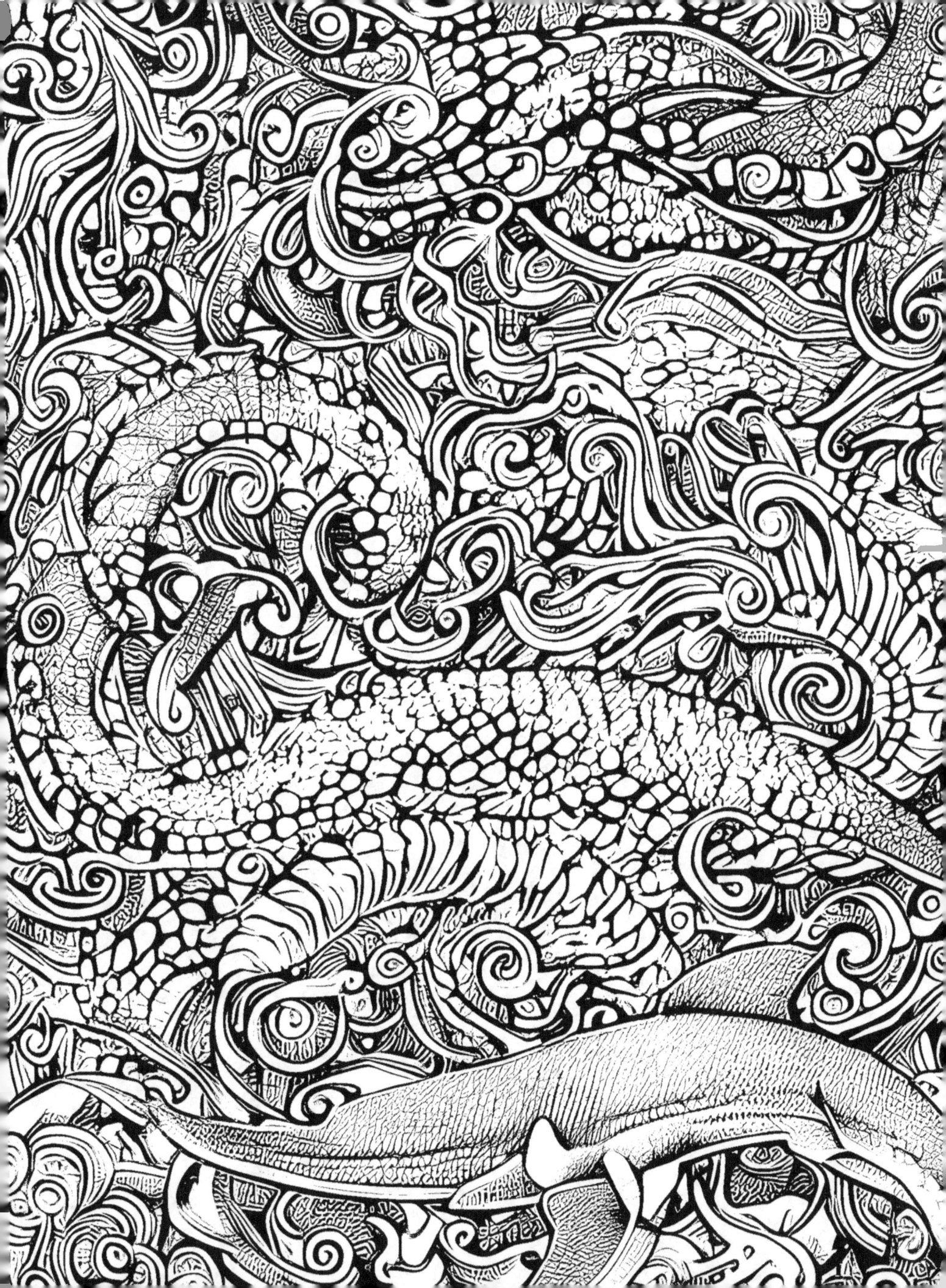

Infinite Ocean

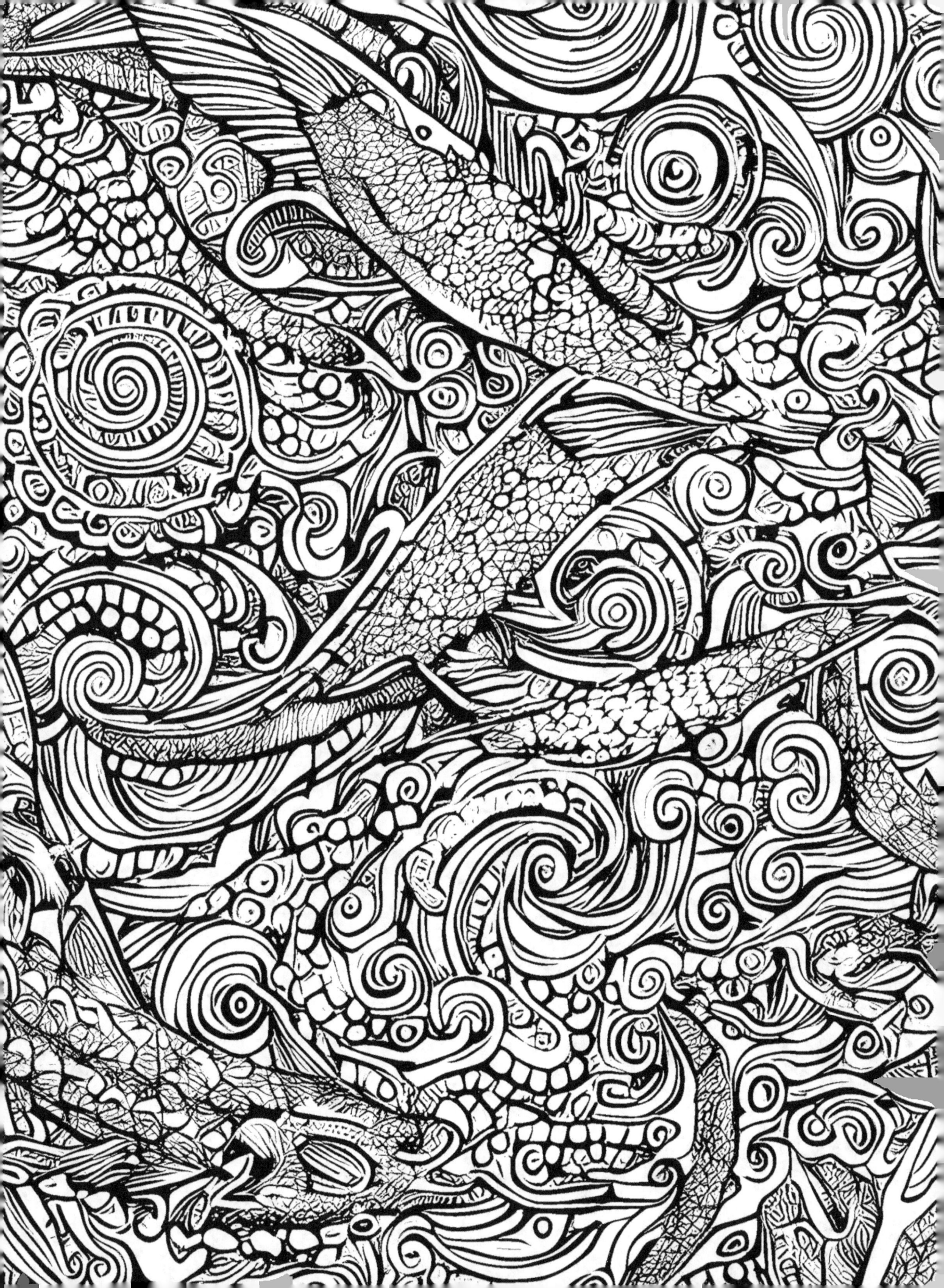

Infinite Ocean

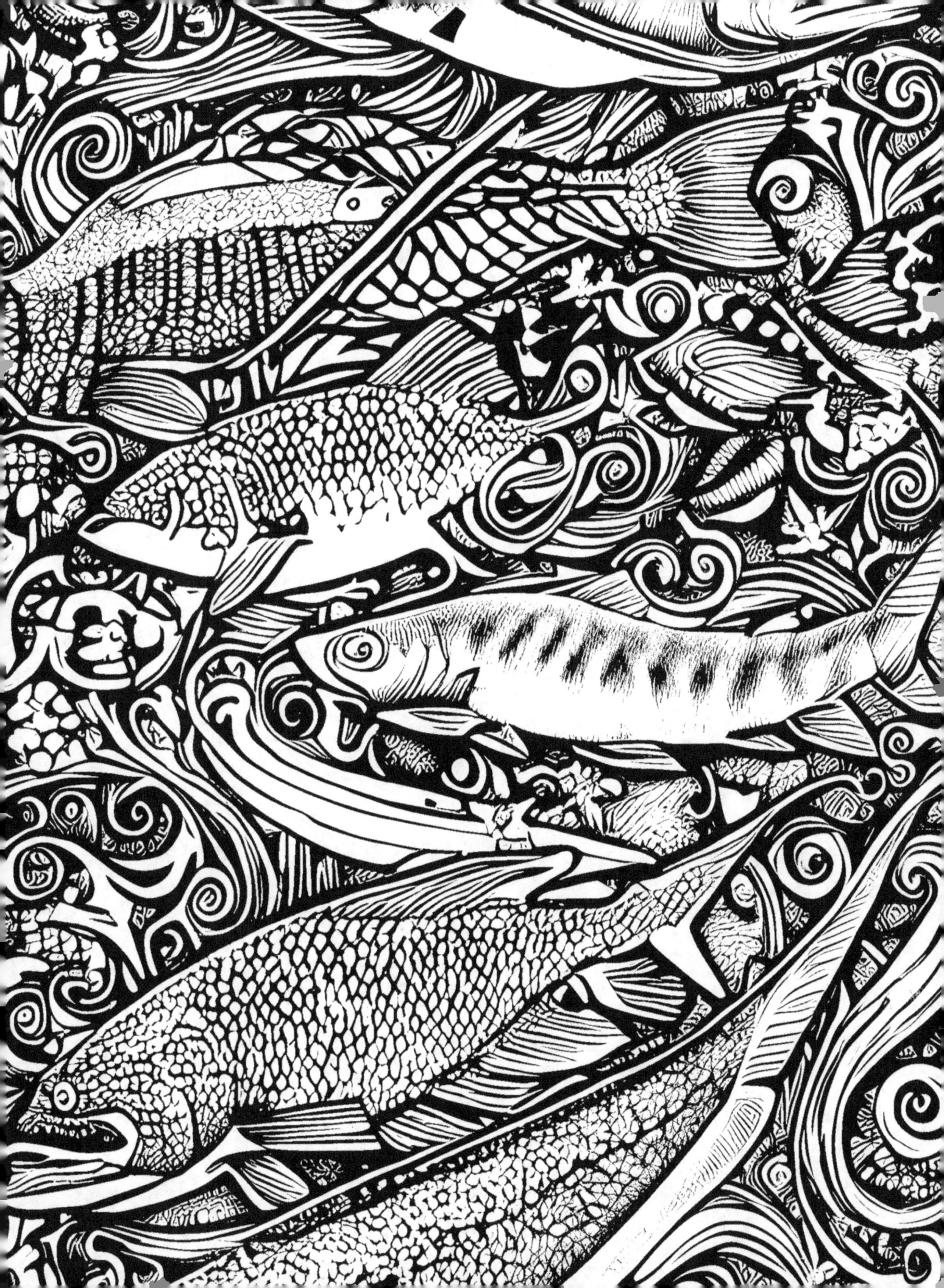

Infinite Ocean

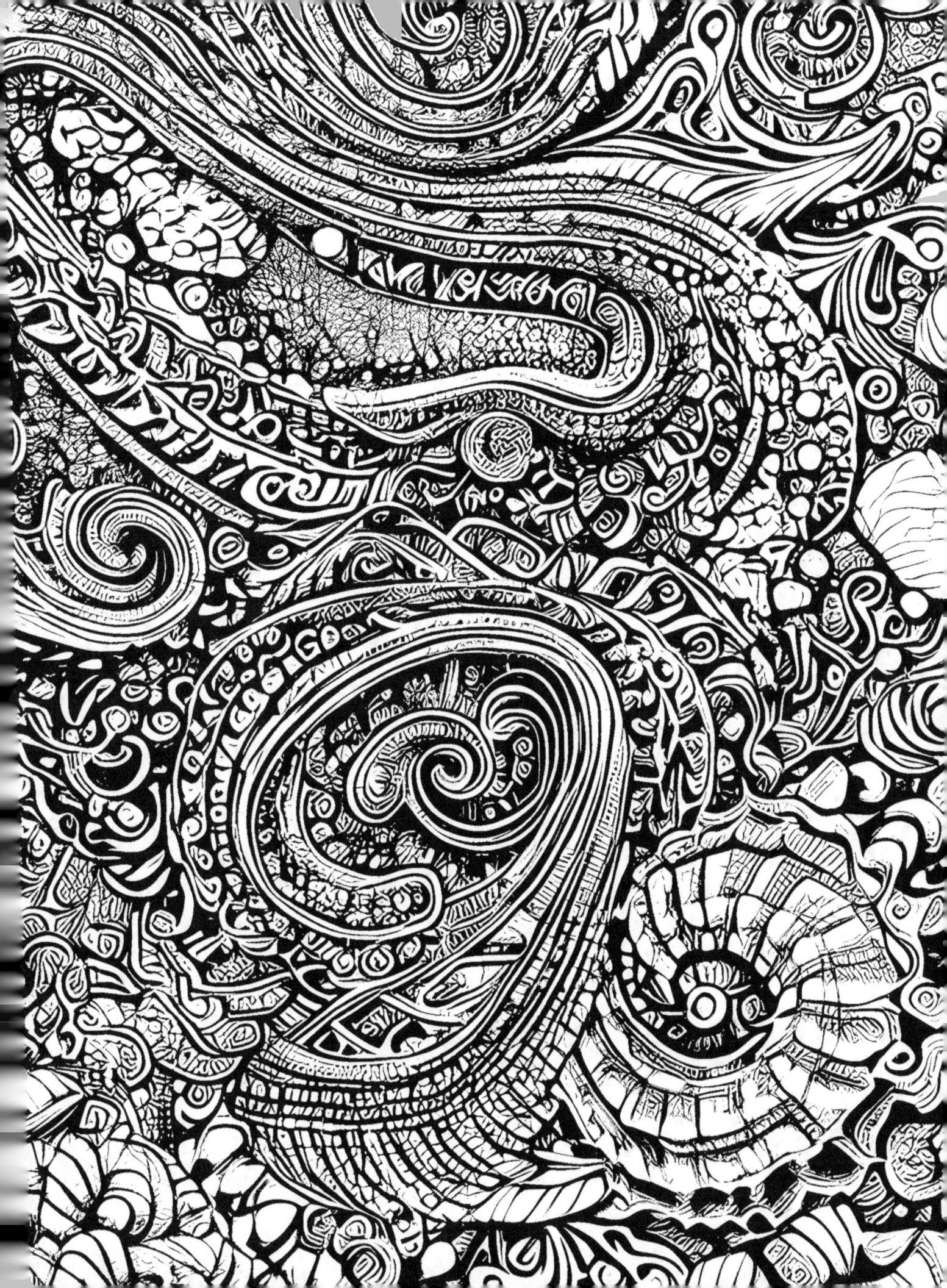

Infinite Ocean

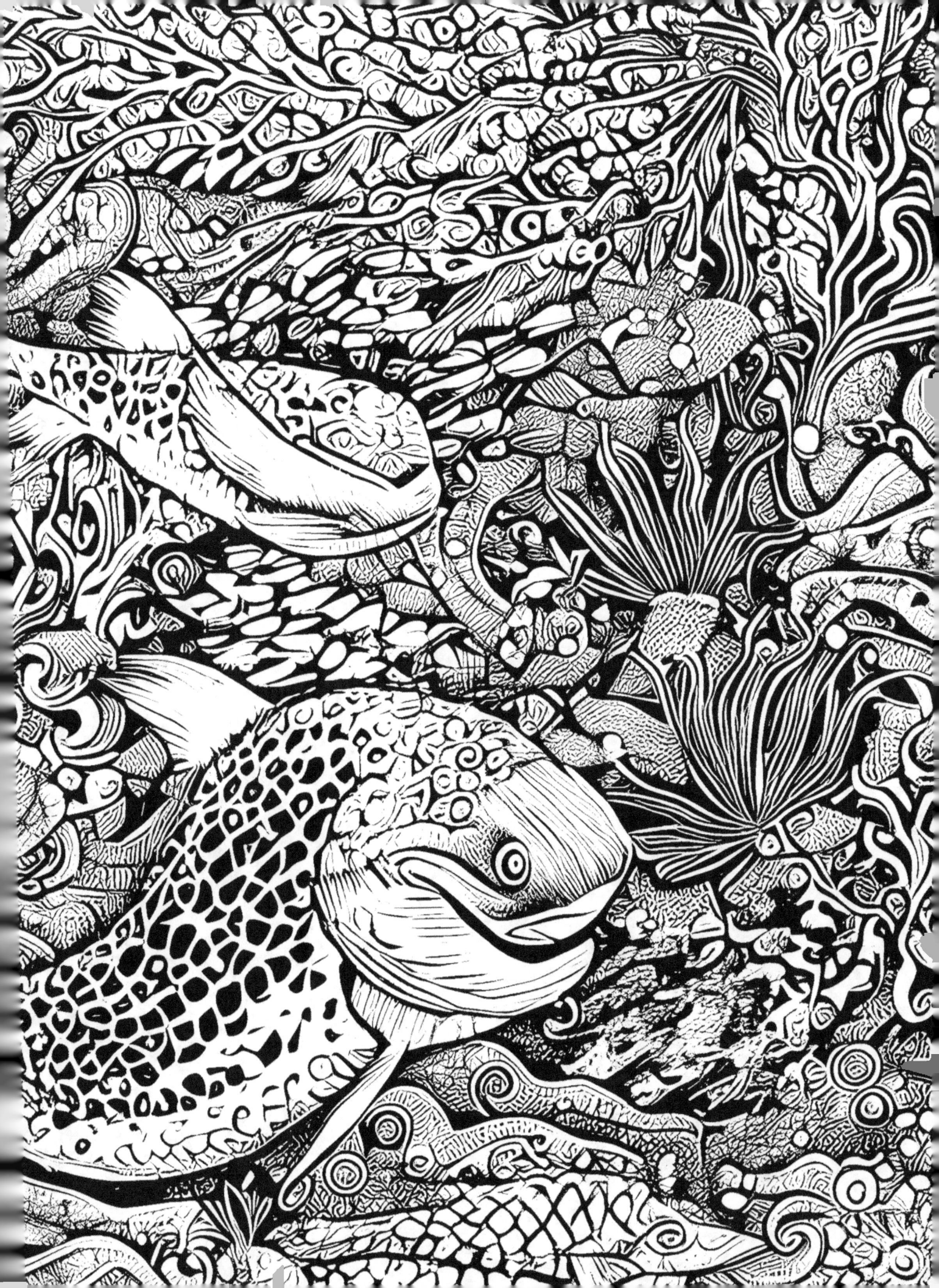

Infinite Ocean

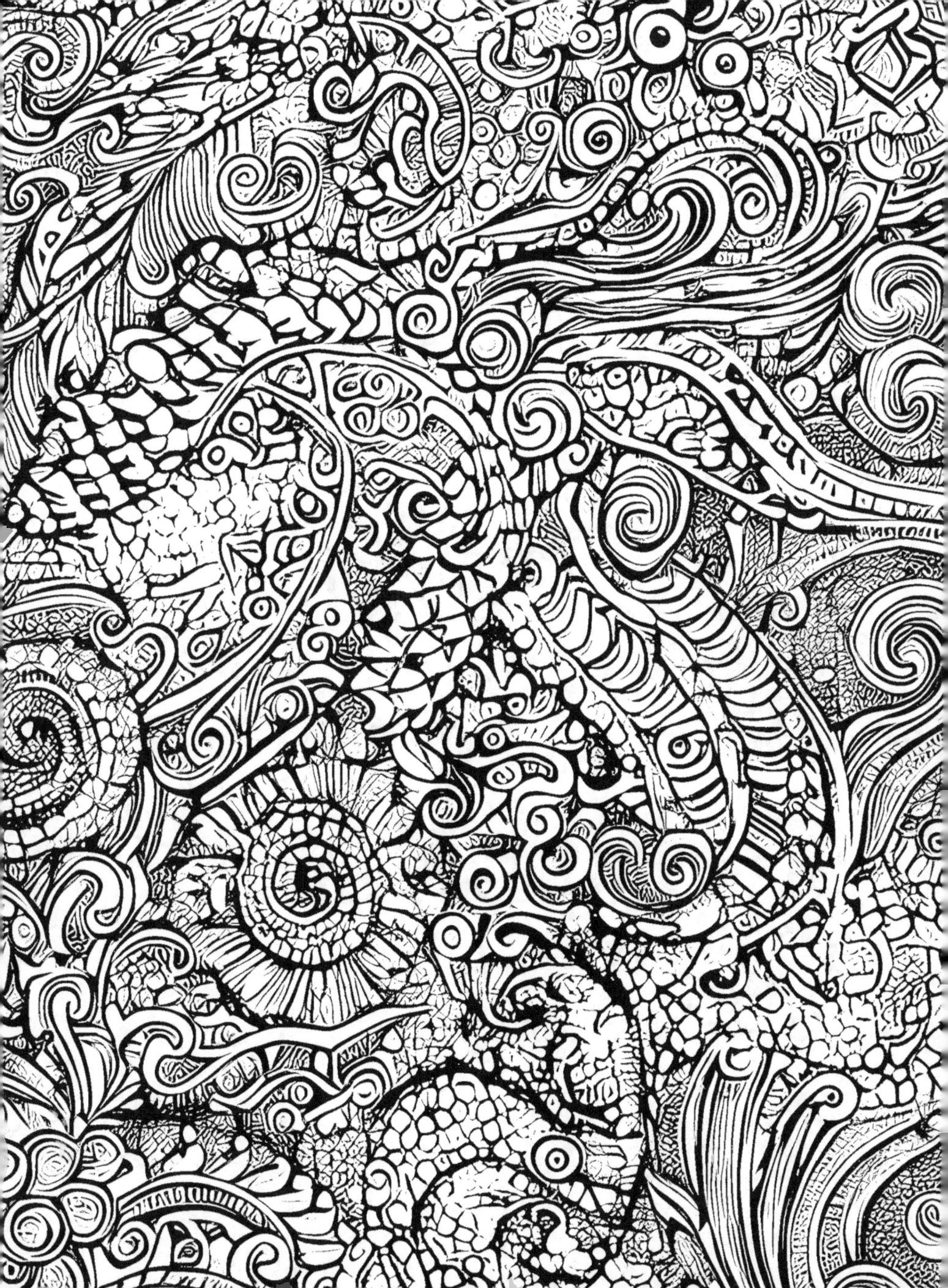

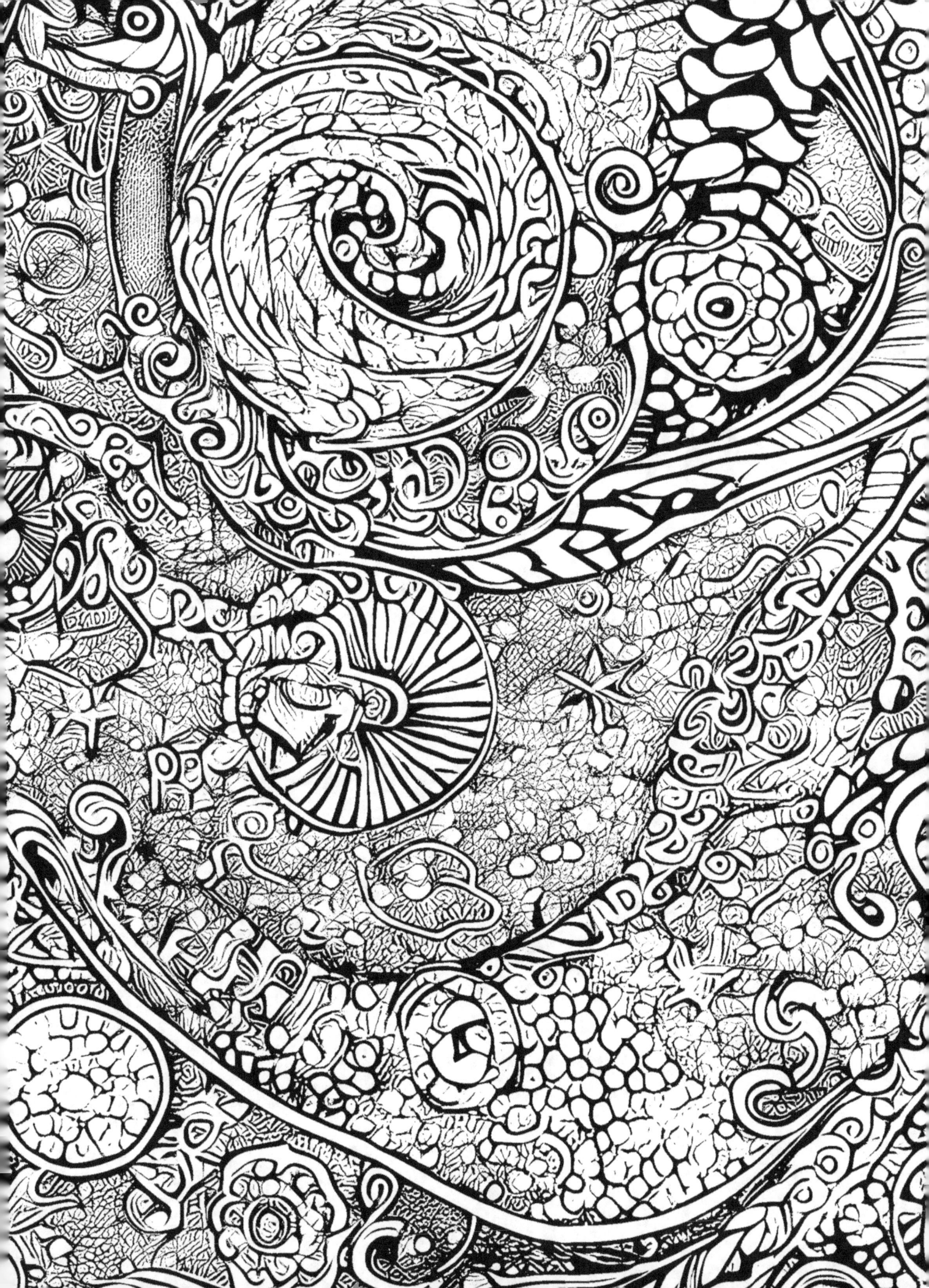

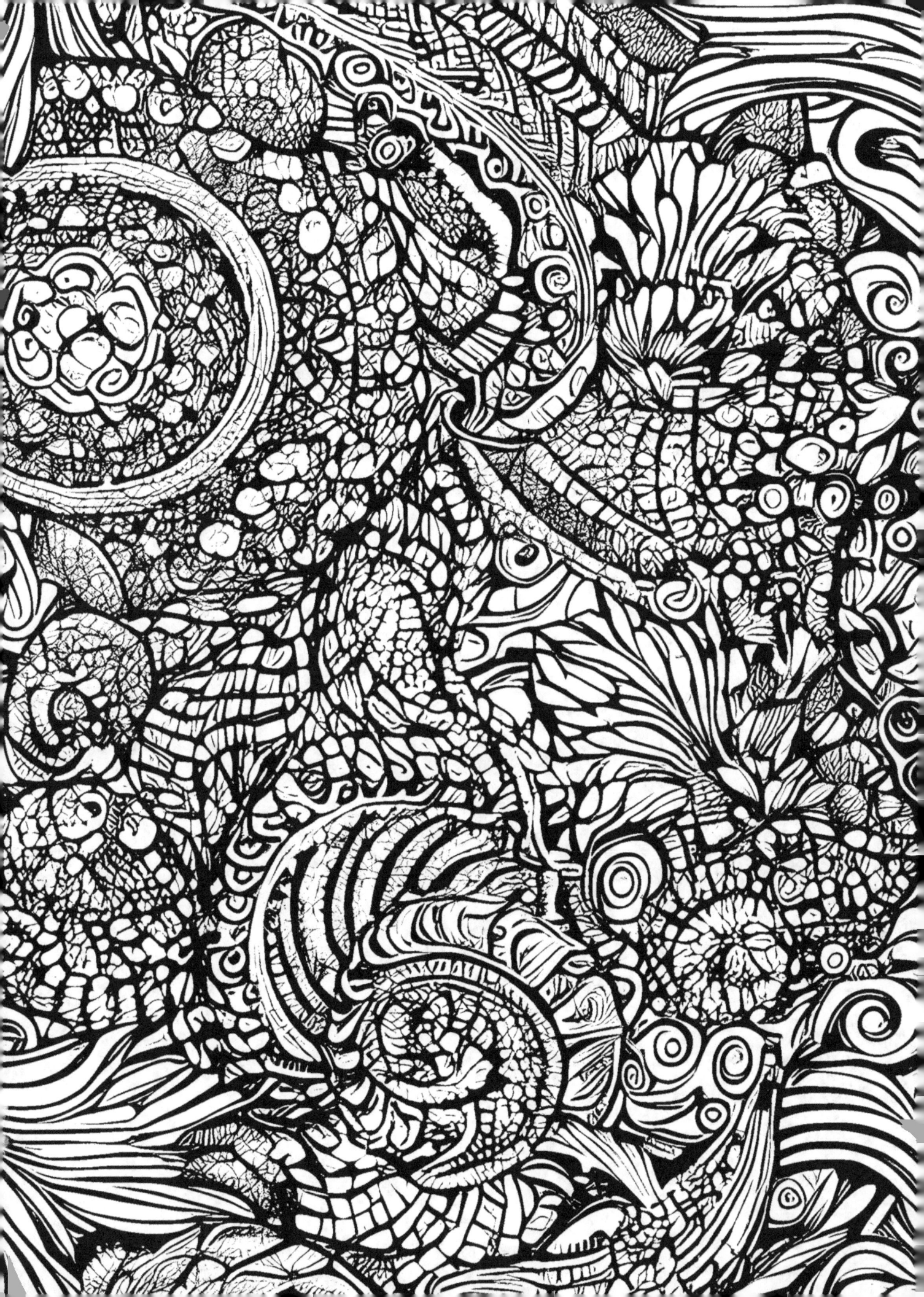

Infinite Ocean

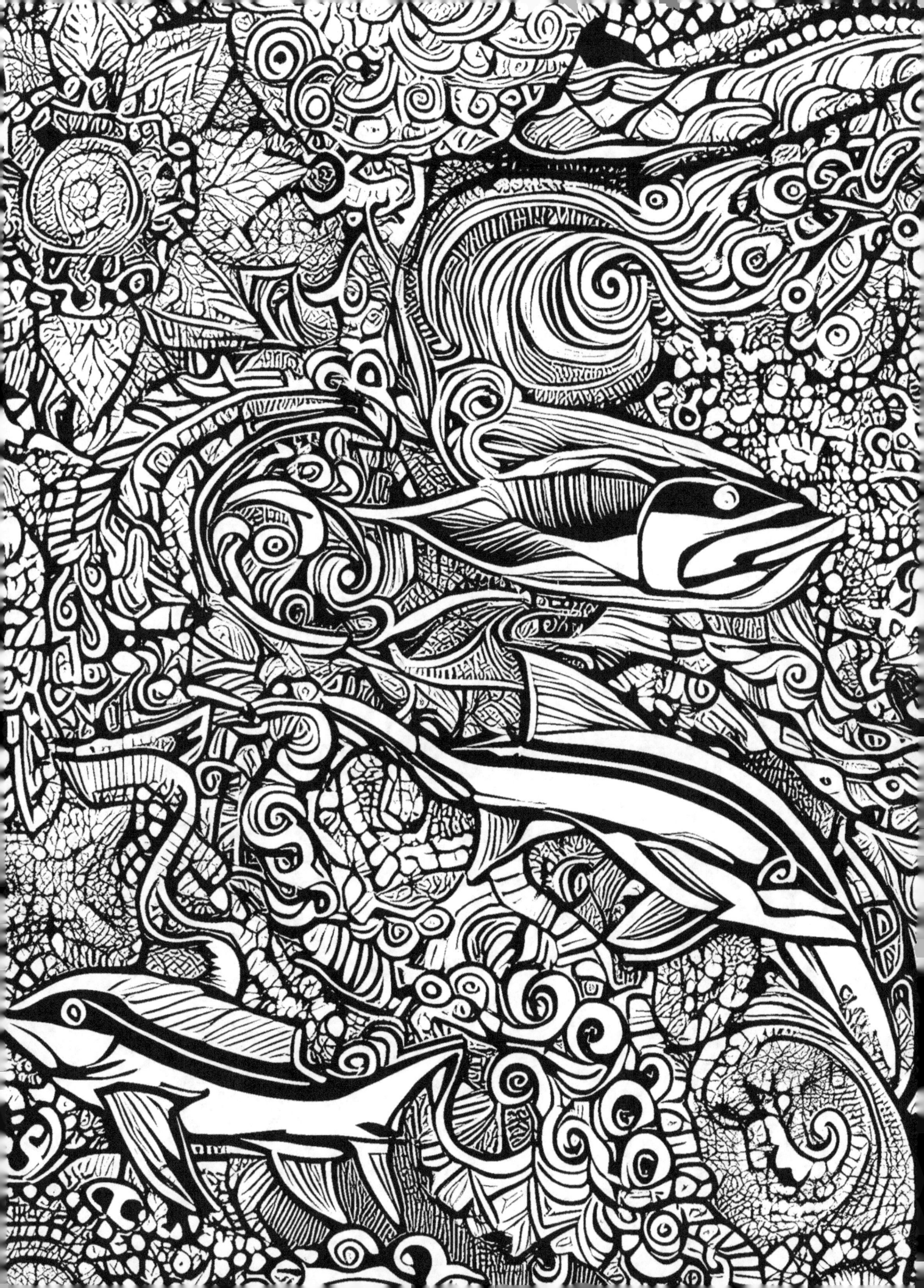

Infinite Ocean

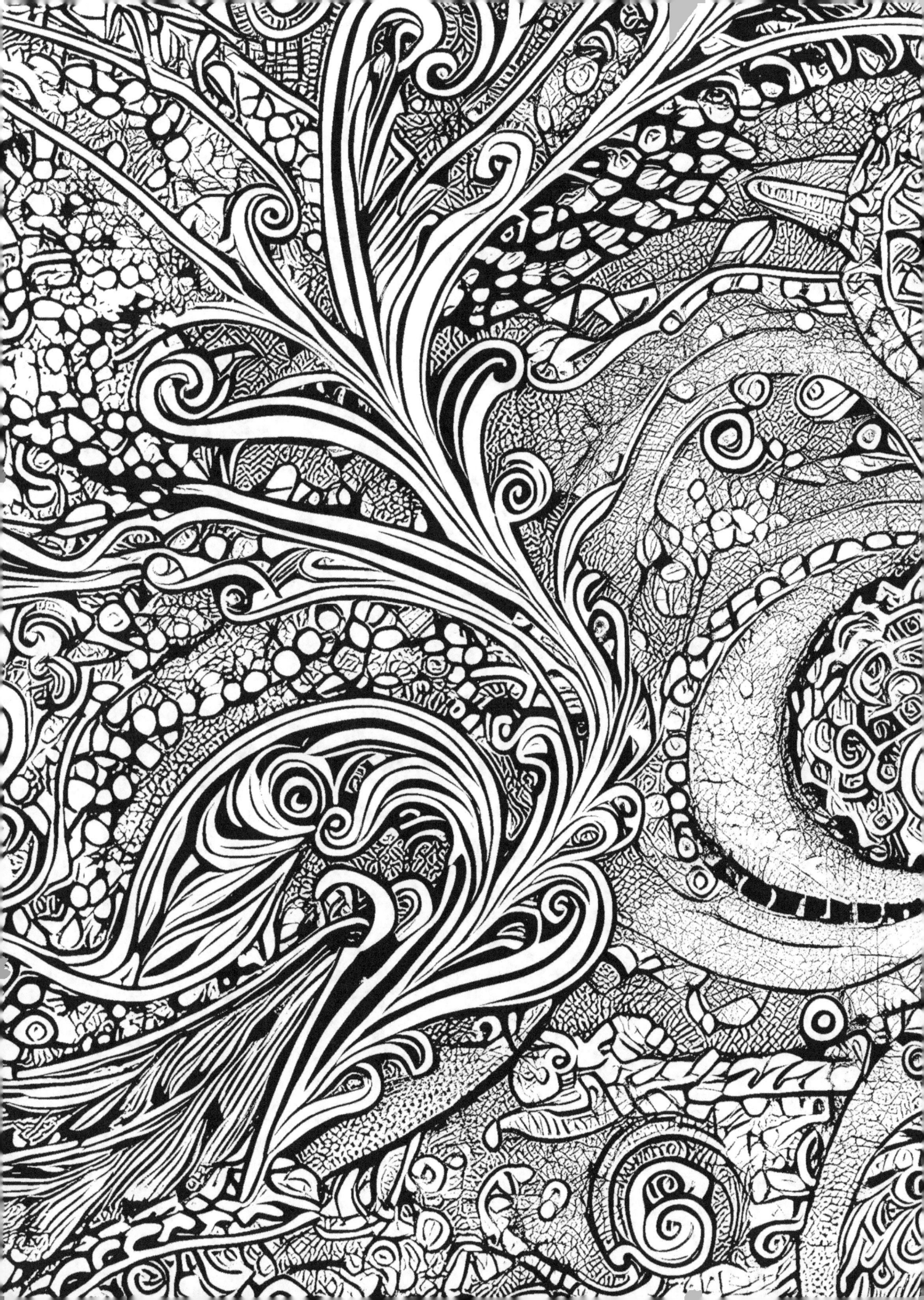

Infinite Ocean

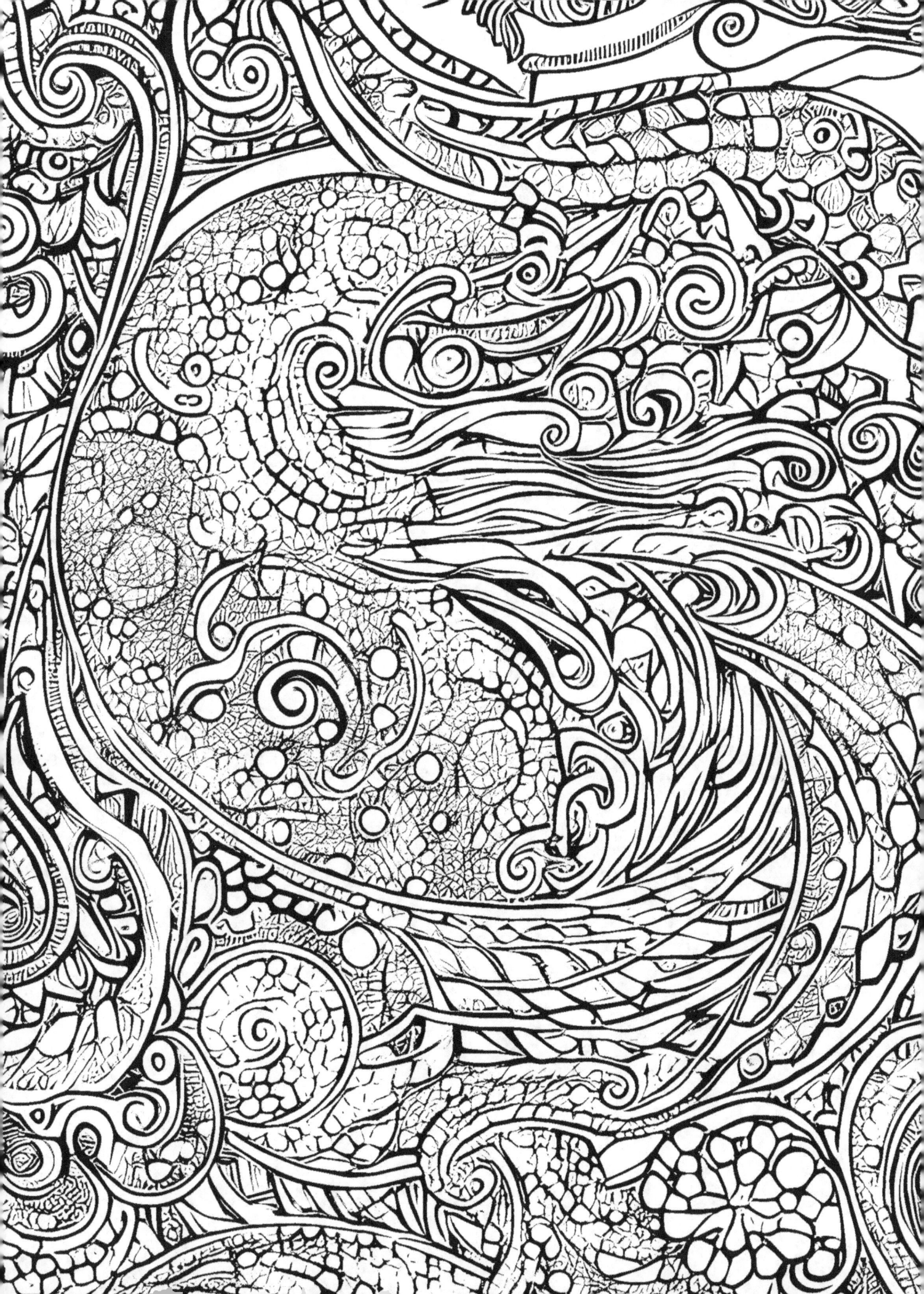

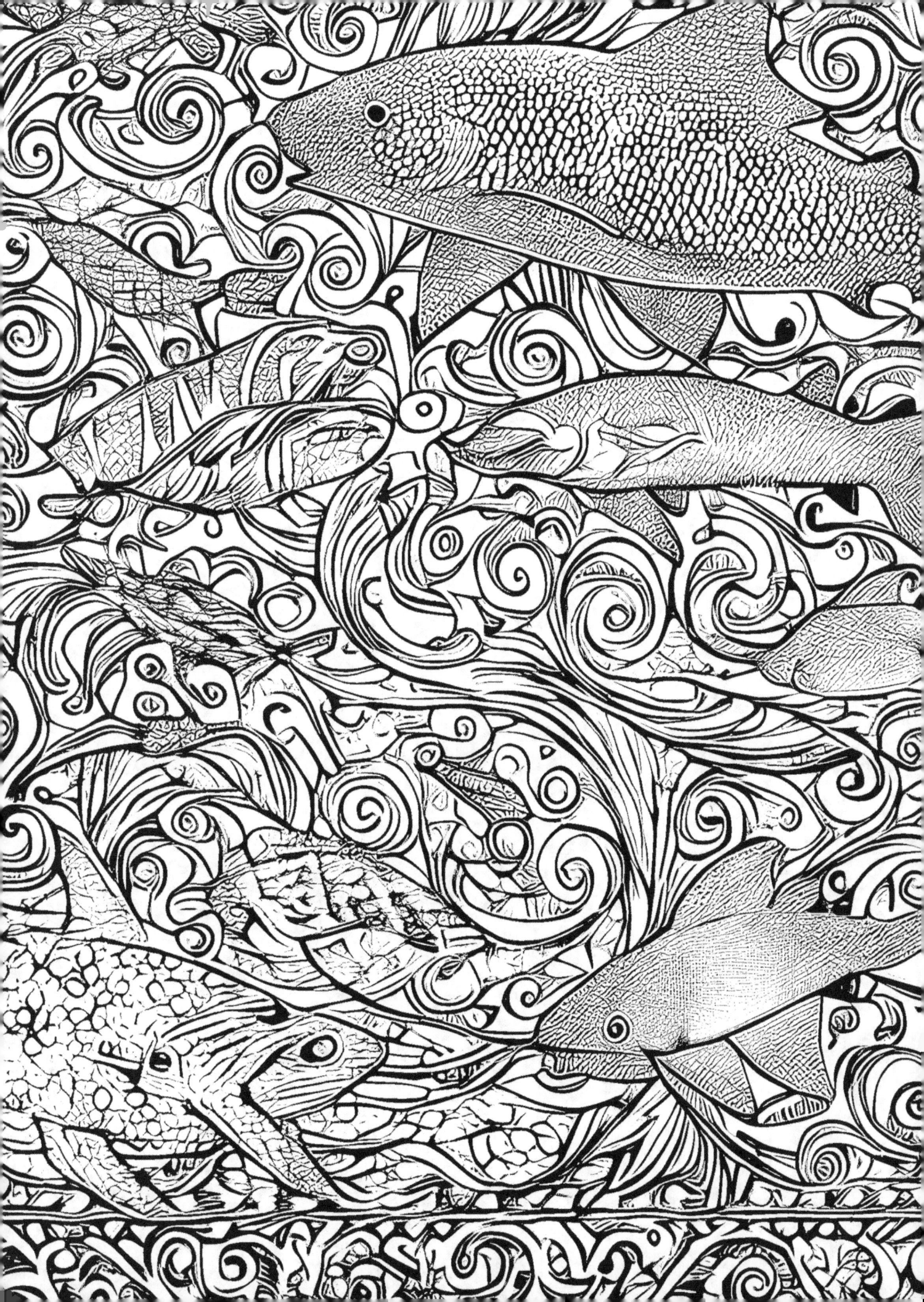

Infinite Ocean

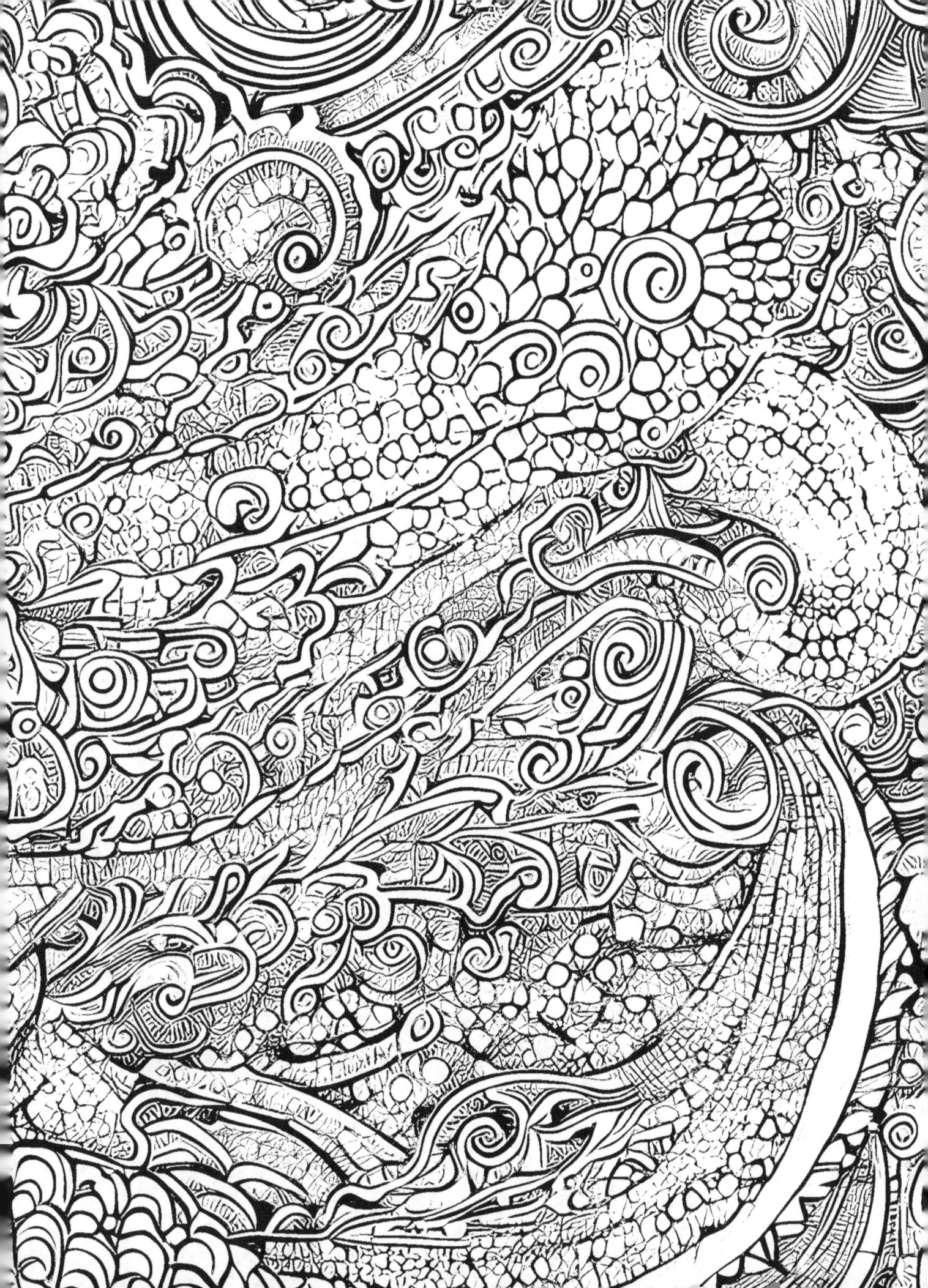

Infinite Ocean

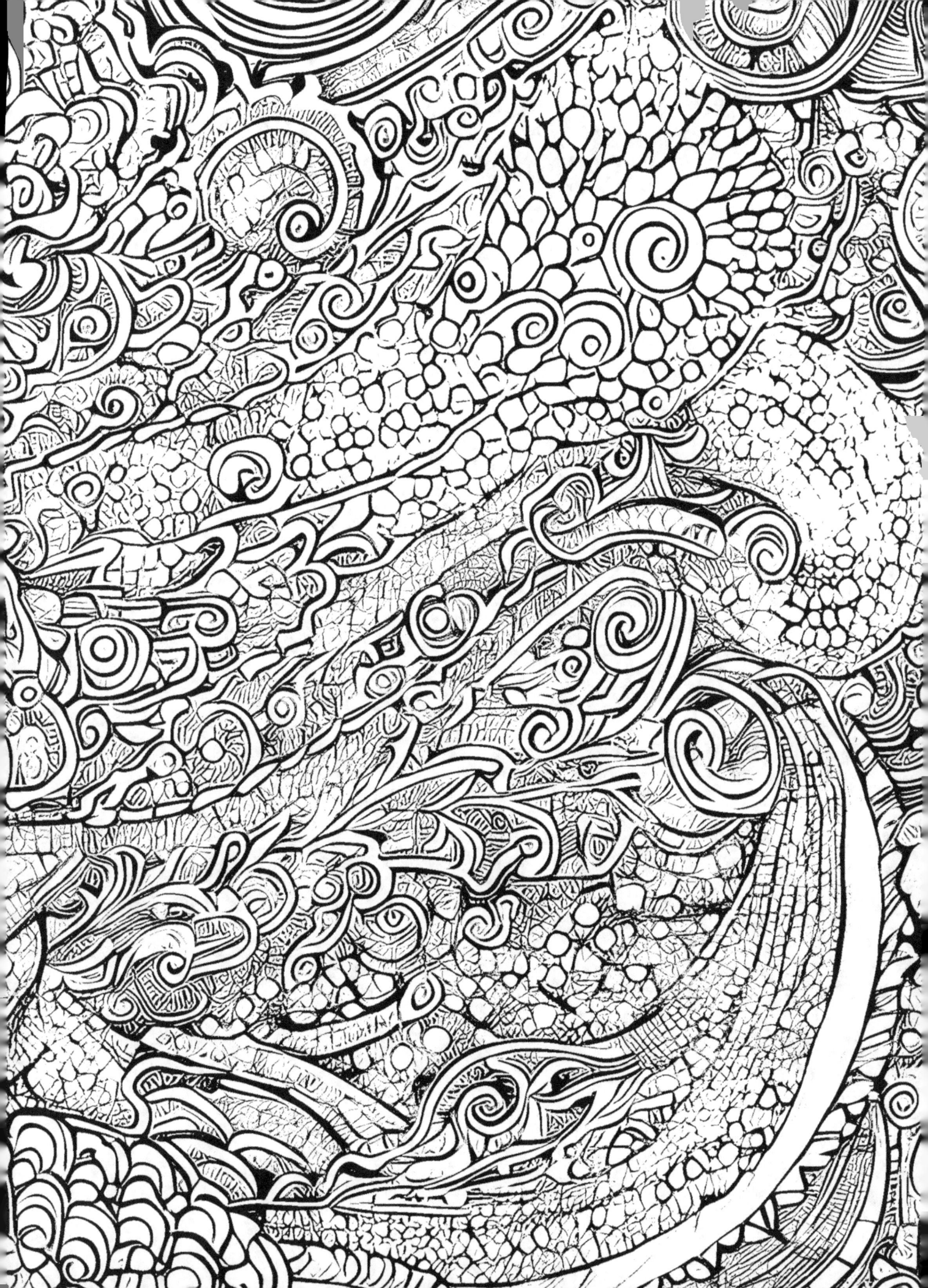

Infinite Ocean

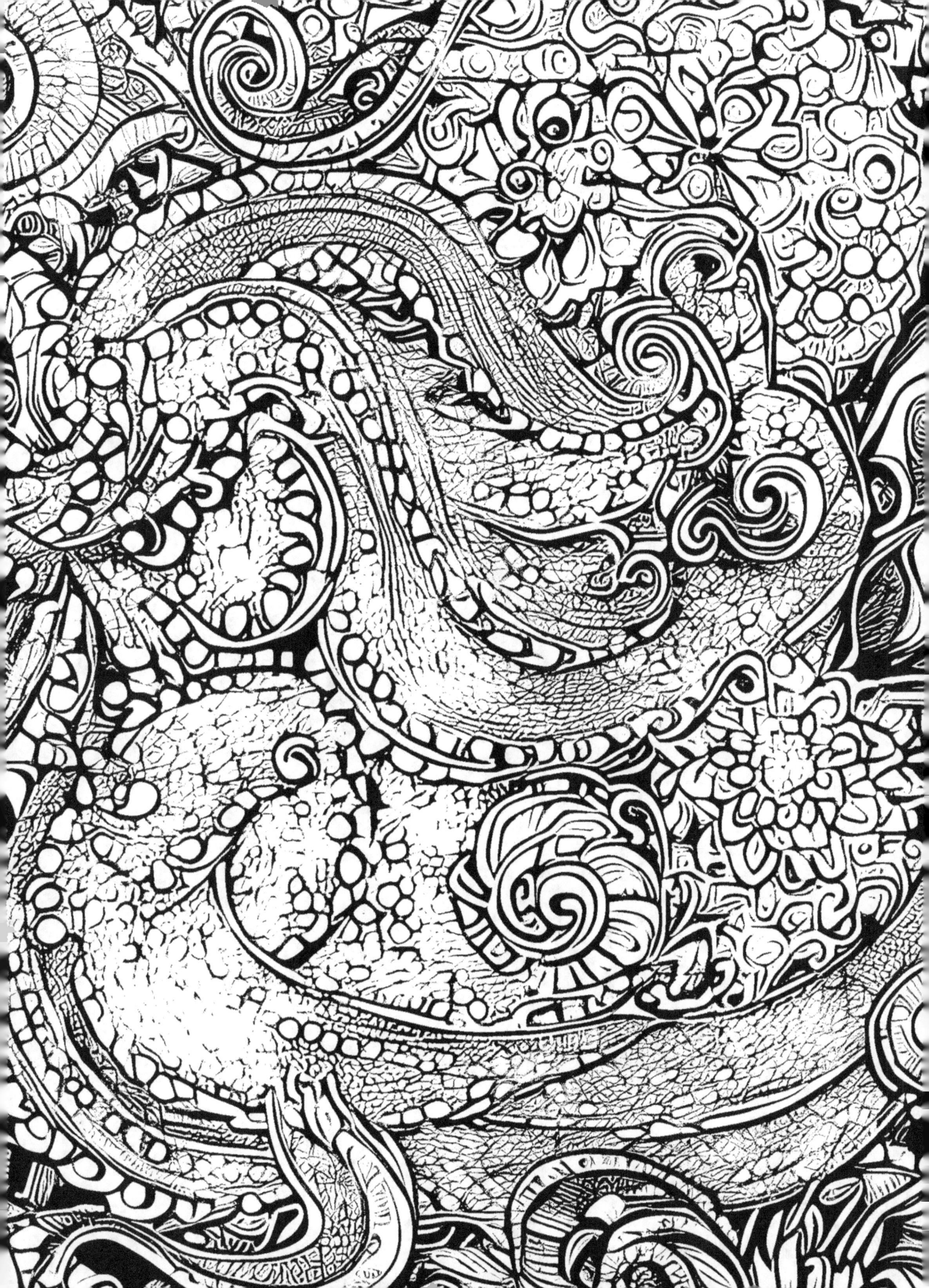

www.ingramcontent.com/pod-product-compliance
Lightning Source LLC
Chambersburg PA
CBHW080517220526
45465CB00006B/2510